Library of
Davidson College

VOID

CAMBRIDGE MUSICAL TEXTS AND MONOGRAPHS

General Editors: Howard Mayer Brown, Peter le Huray, John Stevens

Published

Ian Woodfield: *The Early History of the Viol*

Forthcoming

Robin Stowell: *History of the Violin and Violin Playing from c. 1760 to 1850*

PRINCIPLES OF THE HARPSICHORD
by
MONSIEUR DE SAINT LAMBERT

Translated and edited by
REBECCA HARRIS-WARRICK

CAMBRIDGE UNIVERSITY PRESS

Cambridge

London   New York   New Rochelle

Melbourne   Sydney

Published by the Press Syndicate of the University of Cambridge
The Pitt Building, Trumpington Street, Cambridge CB2 1RP
32 East 57th Street, New York, NY 10022, USA
296 Beaconsfield Parade, Middle Park, Melbourne 3206, Australia

© Cambridge University Press 1984

First published 1984

Printed in Great Britain at the University Press, Cambridge

Library of Congress catalogue card number: 83–7462

British Library Cataloguing in Publication Data

Saint-Lambert, Michel de
Principles of the harpsichord. –
(Cambridge musical texts and monographs)
1. Harpsichord
I. Title   II. Harris-Warrick, Rebecca
III. Les principes du clavecin. *English*
786.3'0421   MT252

ISBN 0 521 25276 8 hard covers
ISBN 0 521 27269 6 paperback

WD

Contents

Translator's Introduction	page	vii
Principles of the Harpsichord		1
Preface		3
Foreword		5
Principles of the Harpsichord		8
I	Concerning Notes and Clefs	9
II	Concerning the Keyboard	18
III	Concerning the Manner of Studying Pieces	21
IV	Concerning Note Values	23
V	Concerning the Dot	26
VI	Concerning the Tie	27
VII	Concerning the Slur	29
VIII	Concerning the Signs that Indicate Meter and Tempo	32
IX	Concerning the Voices	48
X	Concerning Rests	51
XI	Concerning the Double Bar	56
XII	Concerning the *Renvoy*	58
XIII	Concerning the Direct and the *Renvoy*	59
XIV	Concerning Accidentals in General	60
XV	Concerning the Sharp	61
XVI	Concerning the Flat	62
XVII	Concerning the Natural	64
XVIII	Concerning Transposed Pieces	67
XIX	Concerning the Position of the Fingers	70
XX	Concerning *Agréments* in General	75
XXI	Concerning the *Tremblement*	76
XXII	Concerning the *Double Cadence*	83
XXIII	Concerning the *Pincé*	84
XXIV	Concerning the *Port de Voix*	86
XXV	Concerning the *Coulé*	90
XXVI	Concerning the *Arpégé*	94
XXVII	Concerning the *Détaché*	97
XXVIII	Concerning the *Aspiration*	98
Final Remarks		100
Menuet		102
Gavotte		104
Appendix A: Pieces Cited by St Lambert		107
Appendix B: Ornament Tables of Composers Cited by St Lambert		112
Appendix C: Compendium of St Lambert's Ornament Examples		118
Bibliography		129
Index		135

Translator's Introduction

Saint Lambert's *Principles of the Harpsichord*, published in Paris in 1702, is a work of both theoretical and practical importance which deserves to be much better known than it is at present. As St Lambert himself claimed, it is the first true method for the harpsichord, its only predecessors being books about other keyboard instruments or large works about music and instruments with subsections on the harpsichord.[1] As a method book, it contains a wealth of information of interest to performers, including such topics as fingering, the technique of the slur, and ornamentation. But because it is also much broader in scope and covers the fundamentals of music as well, it is a major source for students of late seventeenth-century French music theory. Through this book we see St Lambert as a thorough and sympathetic teacher: thorough in the way he clearly defines the scope of his book and systematically carries it out; and sympathetic in his understanding approach to the differing characters and abilities of his students. Beyond his qualities as a teacher, St Lambert had a streak of the evangelist in him that manifested itself as a desire to systematize and simplify some of the notational practices of his fellow musicians. One of his proposed reforms, a simplification of the system of clefs, was still under discussion at the end of the eighteenth century. Another of his ideas, the systematization of the meanings of the different time signatures, has proven to be of great interest to twentieth-century investigators of the sensitive question of tempo in seventeenth- and eighteenth-century French music. The book as a whole gains still more in interest because of its appearance at a time when the music of the brilliant French harpsichord school was undergoing a stylistic change from the works of Chambonnières and his students, d'Anglebert, Louis Couperin, and Lebègue, to the galant style of François Couperin and his contemporaries. With respect to performance practices, *Principles of the Harpsichord* reflects the attitudes of the earlier period, but as a theorist, St Lambert was among the first to advocate ideas that came into common acceptance in the eighteenth century.

St Lambert is actually the author of two treatises, whose complete titles are:

> Les Principes / du / Clavecin / Contenant une Explication exacte de tout ce qui concerne / la Tablature & le Clavier. / Avec des Remarques nécessaires pour l'intelligence de plusieurs difficultées / de la Musique. / Le tout divisé par Chapitres selon l'ordre des matières.

---

1. Some of the earlier books that contain information about keyboard technique are: Tomás de Santa María's *Libro llamado arte de tañer fantasia* (Valladolid, 1565) which deals primarily with the clavichord and contains the earliest discussion of keyboard technique in any detail; Girolamo Diruta's *Il Transilvano* (Venice, 1593), a treatise on organ playing that includes among other topics an important section on fingering, and also makes a distinction between the techniques of organ and harpsichord; and Marin Mersenne's comprehensive treatise, *Harmonie universelle* (Paris, 1636), which includes extensive sections on instruments, including the harpsichord. There are also a number of 17th-century manuals of thoroughbass realization, both for keyboard and for plucked-string instruments, but these deal primarily with practical harmony and cannot be considered method books for persons learning to play an instrument. For a discussion of these manuals, see F.T. Arnold, *The Art of Accompaniment from a Thorough-Bass* (London: Oxford University Press, 1957).

/ Par Monsieur de Saint Lambert (Paris: Christophe Ballard, 1702),

and

Nouveau Traité / de l'Accompagnement / du Clavecin, / de l'Orgue, / et des autres instruments. / Par Monsieur de Saint Lambert (Paris: Christophe Ballard, 1707).

Both works were published by Christophe Ballard, sole music printer to the king, and were reprinted in pirated editions in Amsterdam by Estienne Roger around 1710.[2] St Lambert also had modest abilities as a composer: two little dances of his own composition appear at the end of the *Principes* and two of the annual volumes from the series of *Recueils d'airs sérieux et à boire* published by Ballard, 1701 and 1702, contain songs of his. He is also the author of at least two poems: one, only four lines long, appears at the end of the Foreword of the *Principes*; the other is an elegant verse in praise of the playing of Louis Marchand, the well-known organist, which appears in Marchand's book of harpsichord pieces, also published by Ballard in 1702. Whether the two men actually knew one another or whether Ballard simply drew upon St Lambert's talents in poetry is unknown.

There has been some confusion surrounding the initial publication dates of St Lambert's two books. Fétis stated that both Paris publications are actually second editions, and that the treatise on accompaniment was first published in 1680, the *Principes* in 1697.[3] Several catalogues and bibliographies refer to the 1702 and 1707 publications as second editions, presumably on the strength of Fétis's claim and despite the fact that F.T. Arnold's discussion of the subject[4] should have settled the matter long since. Arnold points out that St Lambert himself disproves the existence of an earlier edition of the *Principes* by alluding in the preface of the 1702 print to the possibility of making a second edition at a later date (see p. 4).[5] In the *Nouveau traité*, St Lambert says that he feels that his earlier work, i.e. the harpsichord method, would be incomplete without the addition of an accompaniment treatise, a statement which shows that the accompaniment book could not have been published first. As Arnold notes, St Lambert probably included the word *nouveau* in the title of his accompaniment treatise not to indicate that he was updating an earlier

2. The works are listed in a 1712 catalogue of Roger's publications as follows:
Principes pour bien aprendre à jouer du clavecin par Mr. de Saint Lambert
Traitté d'acompagnement pour aprendre à bien acompagner du clavecin par Mr. de Saint Lambert
See François Lesure, *Bibliographie des éditions musicales publiées par Estienne Roger et Michel-Charles Le Cène* (Amsterdam 1696-1743) (Paris: Heugel, 1969), p. 49.

3. F.-J. Fétis, *Biographie universelle des musiciens et bibliographie générale de la musique* (Paris: Librairie de Firmin-Didot, 1878), vol. VII, pp. 371-2. The original error in ascribing the early dates to St Lambert's two books is not Fétis's, at least not for the *Nouveau traité*. The German music lexicographers Forkel (*Allgemeine Litteratur der Musik* (Leipzig, 1792), pp. 326 and 352) and Gerber (*Neues Historisch-Biographisches Lexikon der Tonkünstler* (Leipzig, 1812-14), vol. II, p. 163) both give 1680 as the publication date of the *Nouveau traité*, although they also list the correct date, 1702, for the *Principes*. Walther (*Musikalisches Lexikon*, 1732) was not the source of their information: he correctly gives 1707 as the date of the accompaniment treatise and has no date at all for the harpsichord method. Fétis may have gotten the idea of a 1697 publication date for the *Principes*, however, from a misreading of the entry for Saint Lambert in Gustav Schilling's *Encyclopädie der gesammten musikalischen Wissenschaften* (Stuttgart, 1840), a book which was in his Library: '... Ferner: "Principes du clavecin", und mehrere Trio's für verschiedene Instrumente, die aber, wie jene Principes (1702), erst nach seinem Tode, der 1696 erfolgte, zu Paris erschienen' (vol. IV, p. 308). Fétis himself owned a copy of the 1702 Ballard edition of the *Principes*.
4. Arnold, *Accompaniment*, 900-1. Arnold based his discussion on investigations by Van den Borren and Tessier.
5. Page numbers here and elsewhere refer to this translation of the *Principes* rather than to the original.

work, but to promote his book as the most recent one on accompaniment in relation to the several other accompaniment books already in print. There are also no surviving copies of the purported seventeenth-century editions, nor any contemporary evidence to suggest that they ever did exist. The dates 1702 and 1707 should finally be recognized as the genuine publication dates of the two works.

Nothing is known about St Lambert himself, not even the years of his birth or death. The search for information about him has been complicated by the fact that he has sometimes been confused with the much better-known Michel Lambert (1610-1696), singer, composer of vocal music at the court of Louis XIV, and father-in-law of Lully. Johann Gottfried Walther, for example, has an entry in his *Musikalisches Lexikon* of 1732 under 'Lambert (de Saint)' that lists the complete tables of contents for St Lambert's two books, but also states that he was *maître de la musique de la chambre du Roi* and the composer of an instrumental trio, both of which accomplishments actually belong to Michel Lambert. Other German lexicographers, for example Gerber and Schilling,[6] clearly thought that Michel Lambert and Monsieur de Saint Lambert were one and the same person. Fétis recognized and corrected their error on this point even though he continued to pass on misinformation regarding the publication dates of St Lambert's two books. The frequently seen attribution of the first name 'Michel' to St Lambert, which is not found in any eighteenth-century source, is also probably due to a confusion of the two men.

In marked contrast to many of his contemporaries, St Lambert lists no official titles for himself in either of his two books, nor does he dedicate either of them to a patron or person of importance. The inference to be drawn from this silence - that he probably lacked any highly placed or official position - is supported by the absence of his name from the lists of musicians at the major musical establishments of the period.[7] The only bit of biographical information that he himself gives us ('I had been called to the provinces to teach some persons of quality who wanted to have a master from Paris', p. 15) suggests that he made his living as a teacher, although it is obvious from his accompaniment treatise that he also had a good deal of experience in accompanying both vocal and instrumental music. If he was indeed from Paris, as he claims, he must have been on the periphery of musical life there, or else have been called frequently to the provinces. In his two works he cites a number of seventeenth-century musicians and theorists but gives no hint that he knew them personally. In fact, he seems to have derived all his information about the composers he mentions in the *Principes* - Lully, Campra, Chambonnières, Nivers, Lebègue, and d'Anglebert - from published editions of their works, as he essentially admits when he says, 'I have collected all these *agréments* [i.e. those of d'Anglebert] here, as well as those of the other masters who have had their works engraved' (p. 81). It thus becomes possible to explain the otherwise surprising omission of Louis Couperin from mention in the *Principes* by virtue of the fact that his compositions were not published during the seventeenth century. It is, of course possible that St Lambert chose to mention only works that had been published in order to be sure that his readers would have access to them.

---

6. Ernst Ludwig Gerber, *Historisch-Biographisches Lexikon der Tonkünstler* (Leipzig, 1790-2), p. 777, entry under 'Lambert (Michel)', and the same author's *Neues Historisch-Biographisches Lexikon der Tonkünstler* (Leipzig, 1812-14), vol. III, p. 163, s.u. 'Lambert (Michel de Saint)'; Gustav Schilling, *Encyclopädie der gesammten musikalischen Wissenschaften* (Stuttgart, 1840), IV, 307-8, entry under 'Lambert, Michel'.

7. St Lambert's name does not appear, for example, in the following sources: *Livre commode des adresses de Paris* (1692); Titon du Tillet, *Le Parnasse françois* (Paris, 1732); Yolande de Brossard, *Musiciens de Paris, 1535-1792* (Paris, 1965); Marcelle Bénoit, *Musiques de cour: chapelle, chambre, écurie, 1661-1733* (Paris, 1971); any of the numerous documentary studies published by Norbert Dufourcq and Marcelle Bénoit in the journal *Recherches sur la musique française classique* between 1960 and 1981.

Despite this personal anonymity, St Lambert's two books were quite well known in the eighteenth century. The fact that Roger saw fit to reprint them is one measure of their success, and they continued to be offered for sale for at least half a century.[8] There is also a large number of surviving copies: of the *Principes*, eleven copies of the Ballard edition and eight of the Roger may be found in libraries today; in the case of the accompaniment treatise, there are thirteen copies of the Ballard edition and twelve of the Roger. There are manuscript translations into Italian of both books in the Biblioteca del Conservatorio in Bologna,[9] and the number of citations they receive in the works of eighteenth-century German theorists indicates that they were known in Germany also. Heinichen and Mattheson both cite passages from the *Nouveau traité* in their own books on accompaniment,[10] and Jacob Adlung[11] mentions both books and had obviously read the *Principes*. The portions of the harpsichord method that he cites are the section on ornamentation, St Lambert's proposed reform of the clefs, and the passage regarding the qualities of a good teacher. A number of eighteenth-century French theorists were also familiar with his works. In his *Dictionaire de musique* of 1703, Sébastien de Brossard lists 'le Sr de Saint Lambert' among the 'Auteurs qui ont écrit en François . . . que j'ay vus, lus, et examinez moy-même'. Brossard's close friend Étienne Loulié left among his papers a collection of handwritten observations on a variety of musical topics that include six pages of notes that he had taken on the *Principes*.[12] It is interesting to see what a contemporary as knowledgeable as Loulié found noteworthy. The passages he excerpted in his notes include the difference between the tie and the slur (which definition he termed 'excellent'), a definition of the word *portée* (staff), the chapter on fingering, a substantial portion of the ornament examples (with a comment that St Lambert's way of indicating the altered upper note of a *tremblement* by means of a small flat or sharp above the ornament symbol (see p. 79) is excellent), and, once again, St Lambert's proposed clef reform (see below, p. xiv, for a fuller discussion). Jean-Philippe Rameau without any doubt knew the accompaniment treatise, although he does not say so anywhere: as Philip Gosset has pointed out in his translation of Rameau's *Traité de l'harmonie*,[13] entire passages from the first two chapters of Book IV (on accompaniment) are lifted almost word for word from Chapters I and II of St Lambert's *Nouveau traité* without any acknowledgement as to their authorship.

Although it is impossible to know for certain what impact St Lambert's two books had on their intended audience - the amateur harpsichordist - one indication of their reception may be found in the July 1708 issue of the *Journal de Trévoux*[14] which contains a review, ostensibly of the accompaniment treatise, but in fact of the two books together. The reviewer takes note of St Lambert's statement in the *Principes* that a pedagogical work should be intelligible to the reader without any outside help,

8. Both books are listed in several catalogues of French music dealers during the first half of the 18th century, the latest being from 1751. See Anik Devriès, *Édition et commerce de la musique gravée à Paris dans la première moitié du 18e siècle* (Geneva: Éditions Minkoff, 1976), p. 248.

9. G. Gaspari, *Catalogo della Biblioteca del Liceo Musicale di Bologna* (Bologna, 1890), vol. I, pp. 253 and 340.

10. Johann David Heinichen, *Der Generalbass in der Komposition* (Dresden, 1728; reprinted Hildesheim: Georg Olms Verlag, 1969), pp. 93 and 133; and Johann Mattheson, *Grosse General-Bass-Schule* (Hamburg, 1731; reprinted Hildesheim: Georg Olms Verlag, 1968), pp. 12, 51, 127, 351, 413, 425, 450, 455-6, and 463.

11. Jacob Adlung, *Anleitung zu der musikalischen Gelahrtheit* (Erfurt, 1758; reprinted Kassel: Bärenreiter Verlag, 1953), pp. 212-13, 635, 729-30, and 789.

12. MS Paris, Bibliothèque Nationale, fonds franc., n.a. 6355, fols. 124-126v.

13. Jean-Philippe Rameau, *Treatise on Harmony*, trans. Philip Gossett (New York: Dover Publications, 1971), pp. xii–xv.

14. *Mémoires pour l'histoire des Sciences et des beaux Arts* (*Journal de Trévoux*) (facsimile edn, Geneva: Slatkine Reprints, 1968), issue dated juillet 1708, pp. 1257-61.

even for a subject as difficult to teach through words as music (see the Preface, pp. 3-4) and praises St Lambert as 'perhaps the first author to have written a book about practical music that is comprehensible to readers who had no prior knowledge of the subject'.[15] In speaking of St Lambert's treatment of notation, the reviewer says that 'these things cannot be expressed any more precisely or sensitively. The rest of the *Principles of the Harpsichord* is of the same quality.' The review closes with the wish that St Lambert will someday fulfill the need the reviewer sees for a treatise on practical music that is as well written as the harpsichord and accompaniment books.

In a sense St Lambert had already written at least part of a treatise on practical music in the *Principes* itself: of its twenty-eight chapters, the first eighteen deal primarily with fundamentals of music, although some of the material is specific to the harpsichord. Among the topics covered are clefs, note values, rests, accidentals, and the meaning of such notational symbols as the tie and the *renvoi*. In keeping with his goal of writing a book for people unacquainted with music, much of the material in these early chapters is extremely basic. Chapter III, for example, which bears the promising title 'Concerning the Manner of Studying Pieces', turns out to be a lesson in how to transfer the visual symbol of a note to the correct place on the keyboard. Throughout many of these chapters one gets the impression that St Lambert had spent a good deal of time teaching children; images such as the giant and the dwarf who take a walk together, the steps of the giant representing whole notes, those of the dwarf sixteenths, seem designed to appeal to a child's imagination. The emphasis put on notation in this book may have prompted François Couperin to make a slap at St Lambert's method when he published his own very different book fourteen years later; at least it is certainly tempting to see the opening sentences of *L'Art de toucher le clavecin* in this light.

> The method which I give here is unique and bears no relation to notation, which is merely a science of numbers ... Just as there is a long way to go from Grammar to Declamation, so too the distance from notation to the art of playing well is immense.[16]

It would be an error, however, to dismiss these early chapters as cavalierly as Couperin seems to have done. For those interested either in performing the music of this period or in studying the ideas of its theorists, these chapters contain a substantial amount of useful and fascinating information. In Chapter II there is a drawing of a complete harpsichord keyboard with split keys and a short octave that is an important piece of evidence in helping to establish the usual range of French harpsichords of the period given the fact that there are so few surviving instruments. The chapter on the slur gives this symbol a meaning which has completely disappeared in modern practice and has considerable significance for the performance of unmeasured preludes. Many of St Lambert's notational reforms are proposed in these chapters, and Chapter VIII, 'Concerning the Signs that Indicate Meter and Tempo', contains one of the most important discussions of this crucial topic from the period. Throughout these chapters St Lambert shows himself to be an able and open-minded teacher, tolerant both of the ideas of other musicians and of the weaknesses of his students. If he can be faulted pedagogically, it is for sometimes belaboring the obvious, although perhaps he wrote such passages with a particularly obtuse student in mind.

Of the last ten chapters, Chapter XIX deals with fingering and the

---

15. All translations are my own unless noted otherwise.

16. François Couperin, *L'Art de toucher le clavecin*, trans. Anna Linde (Leipzig: Breitkopf & Härtel, 1933), p. 7. I have slightly modified Linde's translation.

remaining nine with ornamentation. Interestingly, St Lambert reproduces the ornament tables of several prominent keyboard composers from the seventeenth century: Chambonnières, Nivers, Lebègue, and d'Anglebert. By comparing their symbols and terminology and by offering his own views on some of the ornaments, St Lambert gives us a fascinating contemporary look at the French *agréments*. In one particularly interesting case, St Lambert states his disagreement with d'Anglebert on the rhythmic performance of the *port de voix* (see Chapter XXIV). D'Anglebert's ornament table shows the ornamental note played on the beat and dividing the main note in half rhythmically, while St Lambert prefers the ornamental note to be before the beat and of shorter duration. Whereas St Lambert's views seem to be in line with the earlier generation of composers such as Nivers and Lebègue, d'Anglebert's on-the-beat configuration is the predominant one in the French keyboard ornament tables of the eighteenth century. But beyond its historical interest, this dispute shows us an example of that famous arbiter, *le goût*, in action. Clearly musicians' tastes varied, even within the confines of a single style, and the fact that d'Anglebert and St Lambert would have performed d'Anglebert's compositions differently gives us some measure of the flexibility of interpretation in French harpsichord music.

Although *Les principes du clavecin* was published in 1702, the book is firmly rooted in the harpsichord repertoire of the seventeenth century that culminated in d'Anglebert's *Pièces de clavecin* of 1689.[17] Many of St Lambert's comments only achieve full significance when they are seen in the light of the works of composers of this period rather than forced onto the compositions of François Couperin or later harpsichordists. Thus one sees that *Les principes du clavecin* and *L'Art de toucher le clavecin* (1716), although they both represent the French school of harpsichord playing and were published only fourteen years apart, actually relate to different repertoires. They also have entirely different characters: St Lambert's book is methodical and general in that it deals with the practices of a number of different composers, while Couperin's is rambling and highly personal, having as its point of reference the music in Couperin's first two books of harpsichord pieces. For twentieth-century readers the two complement each other and both are indispensable.

The four keyboard composers mentioned by St Lambert - Chambonnières, Nivers, Lebègue, and d'Anglebert - all held official positions in the royal musical establishment and were among the most prominent performers in France. Jacques Champion de Chambonnières (1601 or 1602-1672) is considered to be the founder of the French school of harpsichord playing. He became *ordinaire de la chambre du Roy pour le clavecin* during the reign of Louis XIII and sold the post to d'Anglebert in 1662. At the end of his life he published two books of harpsichord music that contain sixty pieces chosen from among his compositions and grouped by key, although as David Fuller has pointed out,[18] it is very unlikely that these suites were composed as units. St Lambert mentions only the ornament table from Chambonnières's *Livre premier*, but his inexact rendering of Chambonnières's *port de voix* may shed some light on that particular *agrément*, which is confusingly realized in the original table (see p. 88).

Because St Lambert refers so often to d'Anglebert's *Pièces de clavecin*, it is tempting to see him as a disciple of the great harpsichordist, but the references are more probably due to d'Anglebert's stature as a composer and the thoroughness of his treatment of the *agréments* than to any personal relationship between the two men. Jean Henry d'Anglebert (1635-1691), the most eminent harpsichordist of his generation, held the prominent post of *ordinaire de la chambre du Roy pour le clavecin*, having

---

17. The next French publications of harpsichord music were not until 1702.

18. David Fuller, 'Chambonnières', *New Grove* (1980), IV, p. 122.

succeeded his teacher Chambonnières in 1662. His only published work, the *Pièces de clavecin* of 1689, appeared only two years before his death and included four suites, fifteen transcriptions from operas by Lully, six organ pieces, and *Les principes de l'accompagnement*, a brief treatise on accompaniment. Several other pieces of his composition are to be found in manuscript collections, one of them autograph. D'Anglebert's ornament table is the most complete of any French harpsichordist and was enormously influential. Portions of it were appropriated note for note by other harpsichordists such as Gaspard Le Roux, whose ornament table in his *Pièces de clavecin* of 1705 contains only three out of eighteen ornaments that are not copied directly from d'Anglebert. D'Anglebert's table (not François Couperin's, as is sometimes stated) served as the model for the *Explication* that Johann Sebastian Bach wrote out for his son Wilhelm Friedemann in his *Clavier-Büchlein*. In the *Principes*, St Lambert refers to d'Anglebert not only throughout the ornament chapters, but also in the chapter on meter and tempo (ch. VIII, p. 43) in regard to the use of the time signature $\frac{12}{8}$, and in the chapter on the double bar (ch. XI, p. 57), where the reference to two pieces by Lully is undoubtedly to the transcriptions d'Anglebert made of them.

Nicholas Lebègue (c. 1631-1702) may also have been a student of Chambonnières. A player of both the organ and the harpsichord, he was the organist at the church of St Merry in Paris and one of the four organists at the royal chapel. He published two books of harpsichord pieces (1677 and 1687) and three for organ in addition to some sacred vocal music. Only his ornament table is cited by St Lambert, but he is the author of a letter which gives the same meaning to the symbol of the slur as does St Lambert (see ch. VII, pp. 29ff).[19]

Guillaume Gabriel Nivers (1632-1714) was also one of the four organists at the royal chapel. The first of his three *Livres d'orgue*, published in 1665, contains an important preface, cited by St Lambert, which includes information on ornamentation, fingering, articulation, and meter.[20] He is the author of four other theoretical works including *L'Art d'accompagner sur la basse continue* (1689) and the *Traité de composition de la musique* (1667), a work well known to musicians of the period, including St Lambert, who cited it in his accompaniment treatise.

If St Lambert's harpsichord repertoire is retrospective, his ideas on notational reforms were very forward-looking. He was among the first theorists to suggest the addition of another flat to the key signatures of flat keys in the minor mode (see the *Nouveau traité de l'accompagnement*, preface, p. ii). At the time G minor, for example, was always notated as having only one flat in the signature, viewed as it was as a transposition of the Dorian mode onto G. St Lambert recognized that in practice the sixth degree of the scale was minor and should be notated as such in the key signature rather than as an added accidental wherever it occurred. This reform was gradually adopted by composers during the course of the eighteenth century. St Lambert also objected to another vestige of Renaissance notational practice: the use of semi-mensural time signatures (ch. VIII, p. 45). The example he cites is the time signature 3, which by St Lambert's time was commonly understood to indicate a measure containing three quarter notes. Many composers, however, still used 3 as a time signature for the courante or for similar pieces which actually had three half-note beats per measure, instead of using the more accurate $\frac{3}{2}$. In this instance

---

19. For an excellent discussion of the style both of these composers and of the other members of the French harpsichord school, see David Fuller, 'Eighteenth-century French harpsichord music' (Ph.D. dissertation, Harvard University, 1965). Fuller's book on the French harpsichord school is forthcoming from Cambridge University Press.

20. Relevant portions of this preface may be found in translation in appendix B along with the ornament tables of Chambonnières, d'Anglebert, and Lebègue.

too, history was on St Lambert's side, and the old practices gradually died out.

The proposal of St Lambert's that provoked the most discussion during the eighteenth century was his idea to simplify the reading of harpsichord notation by making use of clefs in which the notes would be 'named in only one way' (see the Remark in ch. I, pp. 14-16). From his experience in teaching, St Lambert had observed that the greatest difficulty for beginning harpsichord students was in learning to read the several different clefs in use in harpsichord music; at the time most French harpsichord pieces were notated using a combination of either the soprano and baritone or treble and baritone clefs, but the bass, alto, and French violin clefs were also sometimes used. Since the problem for his pupils lay in the fact that any given pitch, a G for example, was in a different position on the staff depending on the clef in effect, St Lambert proposed notating harpsichord music only in clefs in which the notes would always have the same position on the staff but be simply displaced by octave. The three clefs he chose were the bass clef, the French violin clef, and a clef of his own devising in which middle C was on the second space. In all three clefs G is on the bottom line, but in different octaves. St Lambert went to the trouble of notating several pieces in these clefs and trying them out on children who had not yet learned to read music. The results, he claims, were extremely gratifying. St Lambert was enough of a realist, however, to recognize that his system stood very little chance of being universally adopted, and his pessimism was well founded. Nevertheless, the idea was subjected to a good deal of discussion. Some of the theorists in both France and Germany who thought the idea worthy of notice have already been mentioned. Others paid St Lambert the highest form of flattery by imitating him. Michel Pignolet de Montéclair (1667-1737), composer and theorist, adapted the idea to vocal music with resulting changes in the way of notating octave displacement in his *Principes de musique* of 1736 (see pp. 100–15). He does not mention St Lambert in his book, but Pascal Boyer, writing later in the century,[21] traces the idea from St Lambert through Montéclair to its reappearance in the *Éléments du chant* by the Abbé La Cassagne (1766). Boyer does not object to the idea of eliminating clefs in harpsichord music, but he is strongly opposed to the elimination of a variety of different clefs in vocal music on the grounds that the notes encompassed by the staff when a given clef is in effect have a direct relation to the range of different types of human voices. The *raison d'être* of Boyer's pamphlet is in fact to refute this proposed clef reform and other of the ideas set forth in La Cassagne's book.[22] Boyer cites the *Principes du clavecin* again in the section of his letter devoted to an attack on La Cassagne's proposed reform of time signatures, this time to bolster his own arguments, and it is interesting to find that sixty-five years after it was published, St Lambert's book was still being studied.

The part of the *Principes* that has proven to be of greatest interest to twentieth-century readers is the chapter regarding meter and tempo (ch. VIII, pp. 32ff). In it St Lambert attempts to systematize the levels of tempo as indicated by the time signature and to anchor them to a set tactus in proportion to which all of them move. His system is based on the idea that the time signatures indicate not only the meter of a piece, but its tempo and character as well. In duple meter, for example, the speed of the beat increases by a factor of two in each successive time signature from

21. Pascal Boyer, *Lettre à Monsieur Diderot, sur le projet de l'unité de clef dans la musique. Et la réforme des mesures, proposés par M. l'abbé La Cassagne, dans ses éléments du chant* (Amsterdam and Paris, 1767), pp. 1-5.

22. Boyer's attack prompted La Cassagne to defend himself in print, while other writers joined sides with Boyer. One of them, Jean Benjamin de Laborde, used the entry on St Lambert in his encyclopedic *Essai sur la musique ancienne et moderne* as a vehicle for tracing the development of the idea from St Lambert to La Cassagne in order to condemn it. The article contains no information on St Lambert beyond the titles of his two books. See vol. III, pp. 642–3.

C to ₵ to 2 to $\frac{4}{8}$. Similarly the beat doubles in speed from $\frac{3}{2}$ to 3 to $\frac{3}{8}$ in triple meters, and from $\frac{6}{4}$ to $\frac{6}{8}$ in compound meters. The unit by which these levels of tempo are measured are the steps of a man of average height who walks one and a quarter leagues in an hour, which are equivalent to a quarter note in ₵, 3, and one type of $\frac{6}{4}$. (For St Lambert's own discussion of this system, see ch. IV, p. 24, and ch. VIII, pp. 35-8 and 42-5).

In order to make St Lambert's system applicable to performance, it is necessary to find an approximate metronome value for the steps of his walking man. St Lambert himself indicates that it is faster than ♩ = 60 when he says that 'it is not easy to express in words the length of time that must be devoted to a quarter note, seeing as that amount of time is so small that its measurement cannot be found either in a day, an hour, or even in the smallest part of a minute, for the length of the quarter note is less than all that' (p. 24). In order to make the calculation two values must first be established: the length of the league and the length of stride of an early eighteenth-century Frenchman of average height. As to the league, there were several different leagues in use in France before the Revolution, but the one most probably intended by St Lambert was known as the *petite lieue* or *lieue de Paris* and is equivalent to 2.4222 miles.[23] The length of stride is much more difficult to establish. Today a pace is generally considered to be two and a half feet, but people in the eighteenth century were somewhat shorter than we are. Another possible measure can be found in the pace used by French armies when they marched, which in 1775 was *deux pieds*, or 2.12 feet.[24] Although St Lambert does not compare his walking man to a marching soldier, Pascal Boyer, whose *Lettre à Monsieur Diderot* has already been mentioned, does so, with specific reference to St Lambert. Therefore a stride length of between two and two and a half feet may be assumed to be reasonable. The calculations produce the following results: for a stride of two and a half feet, ♩ = 107; for a stride of two feet, ♩ = 133; for a stride of *deux pieds*, the one that is most firmly based historically, ♩ = 125. This value is, of course, only approximate, but it is supported by Boyer, who claims that European regiments marched at 60 paces per minute for the *pas ordinaire*, and 120 per minute for the *pas redoublé*, and that this last was the equivalent of the steps of St Lambert's man who walks one and a quarter leagues in an hour.[25] A chart

---

23. Ronald Zupko, *French Weights and Measures before the Revolution* (Bloomington: Indiana University Press, 1978), pp. 95-6; and Horace Doursther, *Dictionnaire universel des poids et mesures anciens et modernes* (Anvers, 1840), p. 210.

24. Raoul Camus, 'On the cadence of the march', *Journal of Band Research* 16:2 (Spring 1981), p. 14.

25. 'The duration of the half note has been set at approximately one second; tradition has transmitted this from one musician to another. From another side, and this amounts to the same thing, the quarter note has been assigned the duration of the steps of a man of average height who walks one and a quarter leagues in an hour (see the *Principles of the Harpsichord* by M. de Saint Lambert, p. 10). This is only an approximation, but we have a good idea of it in the essentially inalterable movement of the marches of European regiments. It is known that the airs called marches are in duple time, with a time signature of 2. Thus the whole note, the half note, the quarter note, everything in fact, is determined by this meter. Its tempo cannot be perceptibly altered, because it is based on the step of the troops which, whether by tradition or by a physical constitution approximately the same in all Europeans, is almost mathematically identical from one era to another, and from one country to another.

'What our military men call the *pas ordinaire* is equivalent to the half note; they take two per measure. The step they call the *pas redoublé* is equivalent to the quarter; they take four per measure. It has been observed that the troops take sixty *pas ordinaires* or 120 *pas redoublés* per minute. This relates to the value of a second for the half note which I spoke of first. Thus the marches of the regiments will always transmit to the musician the value that our forefathers assigned to the notes, and will always be able to remind him of the correct tempo of the primitive and fundamental meters, from which he will always be able to deduce the tempo of the other types of meter' (Boyer, *Lettre*, pp. 58–62). Boyer goes on to say that the quarter note has this speed in the meters 2, $\frac{2}{2}$, $\frac{2}{3}$, $\frac{3}{4}$, and $\frac{3}{8}$. The time signature C indicates four slow beats and ₵ is twice as fast. (Unfortunately Boyer never clarifies the relationship between ₵ and 2; it is possible that for him they are virtually the same.) The quarter

showing St Lambert's entire tempo system using the value of 120 to the quarter note in ₵ may be seen in footnote 20 on p. 43.

The basic assumption underlying St Lambert's system, that time signatures indicate not only the meter but the tempo and character of a piece as well, was shared by most of the French theorists of St Lambert's period.[26] It can be seen in writings as far apart in time as the following quotes from Masson (1699) and Rousseau (1768):

> Quadruple meter and duple meter are related to each other in regard to the number [of beats per measure]; however, there is a difference between them in regard to tempo (Charles Masson, *Nouveau traité des règles pour la composition de la musique*, 2nd edn, p. 6).

> Each type of meter has a tempo that is the most appropriate for itself and which in Italian one indicates by the words *tempo giusto* (Jean-Jacques Rousseau, *Dictionnaire de musique*, s.u. 'Mouvement').

The tempo continuum from slow to fast through the various time signatures as outlined by St Lambert can also be seen in French theory of this period, as the following excerpts from a few of the authors who addressed the subject show. Some writers also see a proportional relationship between at least some of the time signatures.

Masson, *Nouveau traité* (2nd edn, 1699):
Quadruple meter may be beaten in two sorts of tempo, that is a slow note beat is faster than 120 in $\frac{6}{4}$, $\frac{9}{4}$, and $\frac{12}{4}$, and $\frac{6}{8}$, $\frac{9}{8}$, and $\frac{12}{8}$ are twice as fast as the preceding three (pp. 63-6).

26. See Eugène Borrel, *L'interprétation de la musique française* (Paris, 1934; reprinted AMS Press, 1978), pp. 163-83 for a discussion of some of the sources, including St Lambert, that express this idea. Others omitted by Borrel include Nivers (see the preface to his book of organ pieces in appendix B) and Hotteterre, *L'Art de préluder sur la flûte traversière, sur la flûte-à-bec, sur le haubois, et autres instrumens de dessus* (Paris, 1719; reprinted Paris: A. Zurfluh, 1966), pp. 66-70.

tempo [in which case the time signature is C, as the ensuing discussion makes clear] or a quick tempo [₵].

Duple meter may be beaten in four sorts of tempo, that is a slow tempo [i.e. ₵], a quick tempo [2], fast [also 2], and very fast [$\frac{8}{4}$].

Fast quadruple meter is the same as slow duple meter, for one beat of the slow meter lasts two beats of the duple meter. (pp. 6-7)

Hotteterre, *L'Art de préluder* (1719):
Quadruple meter is indicated by a C. It is composed of four quarter notes or the equivalent and is usually beaten very slowly. (p. 66)

The [next] meter is indicated by ₵. Like the preceding one it is composed of four quarter notes ... Its usual movement is four quick beats or two slow beats ... One may conclude that this meter occupies the middle between quadruple meter indicated by C and duple meter indicated by a simple 2. (pp. 66-7)

This meter is indicated by a simple 2 ... It is usually lively [*vive*] and *piqué* ... If it is used in slow pieces, there must be some indication given. One may say that this meter is properly that of C divided in two and with the eighth notes changed into quarter notes. (p. 67)

Loulié, *Elements or Principles of Music* (1696), trans. A. Cohen:
In every meter signature, whatever it be, the beats should be more or less slow in proportion to the value of each time [unit].

For example, $\frac{3}{1}$ should be beaten more slowly than $\frac{3}{4}$, because the beat in $\frac{3}{1}$ has the value of a whole note, and in $\frac{3}{4}$ that only of a quarter note. (p. 28)

Montéclair, *Principes de musique* (1736):
The meter designated by $\frac{3}{2}$ ... is beaten in three slow beats.

The meter indicated by $\frac{3}{4}$ ... is beaten in three quick beats.

The meter indicated by $\frac{3}{8}$ ... is beaten in three; but since eighth notes have half as much value as quarter notes, this meter is beaten twice as fast as the preceding one. (p. 26)

St Lambert's contribution to the theory of meter was to extend such ideas into an entire system based on strict proportional relationships between the time signatures and anchored to a definable pulse, his walking man. His proposals were made in reaction to 'the imprecise meaning of the time signatures', which he regarded as 'a defect in the art [of music]' (p. 45). But as is so often the case, contemporary practice was much too unruly to fit itself into such a neat theoretical construct, even when the basis for it was solid. The most obvious problem with the system is that it fails to take into account the different levels of tempo within a given time signature. The dance types sarabande, passacaille, chaconne, and menuet, for example, are all generally notated with the time signature 3, yet were performed at very different speeds, as an abundance of evidence from the period shows.[27] St Lambert himself recognized the phenomenon, as may be seen from his statement that the menuet should be performed as if it were notated in $\frac{3}{8}$, and from a musical example with the time signature 3 that bears the indication *lentement* (see p. 93), but his generalizing impulses seem to have gotten the better of him.[28] Other theorists made a distinction between meter [*mesure*] and tempo [*mouvement*]:

Meter and tempo are different things. We have an example of this in the Minuet and in the Sarabande, which are in the same triple meter, the tempo of the Minuet being much faster than that of the Sarabande. (Loulié, *Elements*, Cohen trans., p. 26)

Meter and tempo must not be confused as they are two different things, since the same time signature is beaten sometimes slowly and sometimes quickly. (Montéclair, *Principes*, p. 21)

Another question posed by St Lambert's explanations is the accuracy of his statement that the half note beat in 2 is twice as fast as the half note in ₵. The question has obvious relevance for performance, particularly in musical contexts where the meter changes frequently, as in recitative, or in scenes within operas where pieces in different meters succeed one another. Certainly a large number of theorists, among them Jean Rousseau,[29] Loulié, Masson, Hotteterre, Démoz de la Salle,[30] and Montéclair, agree that 2 is faster than ₵, but they either fail to say by how much or regard both time signatures as subject to variation in tempo depending on their context.[31] Others, however, imply either that there was no difference between them or that certain musicians ignored the distinction.

27. See Neal Zaslaw, 'Materials for the life and works of Jean-Marie Leclair l'aîné' (Ph.D. dissertation, Columbia University, 1970), pp. 238-367; and Robert Donington, *The Interpretation of Early Music*, new version (London: Faber & Faber, 1974), pp. 382-434.

28. Perhaps in this section St Lambert was following his own dictum (p. 6) that a good teacher 'reveals his principles methodically and always presents them in the form of simple and isolated ideas ... He teaches a general rule as if it were without exception, waiting for an occasion to produce this exception before speaking about it.'

29. Jean Rousseau, *Méthode claire, certaine et facile pour aprendre à chanter la musique* (4th edn, Amsterdam, 1691), p. 35.

30. Démoz de la Salle, *Méthode de musique* (Paris, 1728), pp. 149-70.

31. Pascal Boyer, who as late as 1767 agreed with St Lambert that time signatures not only had implications for tempo, but that there was a tempo norm for the quarter note in proportion to which all the time signatures moved, described how time words could be used to modify the tempo implied by the time signature. Musicians, he said, had a choice, between any two meters, of either slowing down the tempo of the one that was twice as fast, or speeding up the tempo of the one that was twice as slow. For example, to obtain a tempo somewhere between the natural tempos of $\frac{3}{4}$ and $\frac{3}{8}$ one could either add the word *légèrement* or something similar to the time signature $\frac{3}{4}$, or add *modérément* to the time signature $\frac{3}{8}$. But in no case should the time signature $\frac{3}{4}$ ever be pressed beyond the natural tempo of $\frac{3}{8}$, and conversely, $\frac{3}{8}$ slowed down should always remain above the tempo for $\frac{3}{4}$, 'even if only for the thousandth part of a second' (*Lettre*, pp. 66-8).

The two beats of the minor time signature [₵] or of the binary time signature [2] are usually worth no more than two beats of the major time signature [C]. [I.e. a half note in ₵ or 2 is approximately equal to a quarter note in C.] (Nivers, *Livre d'orgue* [1665], preface)

Monsieur de Lully used this meter [₵] in his operas fairly indifferently with that of 2. (Hotteterre, *L'Art de préluder*, p. 67)

There is also the lone testimony of Georg Muffat, a German composer who spent some time in Paris studying Lully's style, that 2 is a little slower than ₵:

> The beat or measure governed by the signs 2 and ₵, divided into two parts, must be given once again as fast as that following the sign C, divided into four. Moreover, the time of those pieces comprehended by the names Ouverture, Prelude, and Symphonie is to be beaten rather slowly when it is marked 2, a little more briskly for the Ballet, in any case more slowly than one beats at the sign ₵, which last, in the Gavotte, is not so precipitate as in the Bourée.[32]

A thorough study remains to be undertaken of the actual use to which time signatures were put in the music of the composers of this period, although some attention has been given to the problem of recitative.[33] An examination made by Neal Zaslaw of the correlation between time signature and tempo in the gavottes of the violinist Jean-Marie Leclair *l'aîné* (1697-1764) reveals that with very few exceptions Leclair used ₵ for gavottes at a slower tempo (as determined by the time words added by the composer) and 2 for livelier ones.[34] Further studies of this kind could help clarify the relationship of meter and tempo in actual practice.

Another problematic result of St Lambert's proportional scheme is the wide difference in the speed of the eighth note between the meters $\frac{3}{8}$ and $\frac{6}{8}$. Although there are some indications that $\frac{6}{8}$ implied a faster tempo for the eighth note than $\frac{3}{8}$,[35] the end result of doubling the speed of the beats in 3 and in $\frac{6}{4}$ is an eighth note which goes three times faster in $\frac{6}{8}$ than the eighth note in $\frac{3}{8}$, a tempo that seems excessive, to say the least. In this instance St Lambert's desire to arrange his material into a beautifully symmetrical system seems to have interfered with his common sense. Perhaps in constructing his system St Lambert was reacting to the breakdown of the Renaissance tactus tradition by trying to re-establish order in what he saw as the confusion of contemporary musical practice. Certainly he was only too aware of his position as the voice crying in the wilderness:

> From all this I conclude that since people are so inexact in music in observing the rules of time signatures and tempo, the reader who studies the principles of the harpsichord here should not dwell very much on everything I have said on the subject. He may avail himself of the musician's privilege and give pieces whatever tempo pleases him without paying more than passing attention to the time signature which marks it, *provided that he not choose a tempo opposite to the one demanded by the time signature*, which could remove all grace from the piece, but rather that he choose one which is appropriate and shows the piece to advantage. (p. 45, italics added)

The last part of the sentence is, of course, what sends us back to study-

---

32. Georg Muffat, Foreword to *Florilegium Primum* (Augsburg, 1695), as translated in Oliver Strunk, *Source Readings in Music History* (New York: W.W. Norton & Co., 1950), p. 444.

33. See R. Peter Wolf, 'Metrical relationships in French recitative of the 17th and 18th centuries', *Recherches sur la musique française classique* 18 (1978), 29-49.

34. Zaslaw, 'Leclair', pp. 246-7.

35. See, for example, Montéclair, *Principes de musique*, p. 42: 'The meter $\frac{6}{8}$ is more appropriate for canaries and passepieds than is $\frac{3}{8}$, on account of the fast tempo [*vitesse du mouvement*] that these two airs require.'

ing both St Lambert's earlier statements about tempo and the observations of other musicians on the subject. St Lambert did not pull his ideas on tempo out of thin air but based them on a long tradition of both theory and practice. Since we are unable to listen in on an eighteenth-century concert, we have to make do with written accounts, imperfect as they are, and with the testimony of the music itself. St Lambert recognized that 'music cannot easily be taught through writing, since that which relates to execution must almost of necessity be demonstrated orally or by hand', yet we must be grateful to him for trying, for his book has a great deal to reveal to us about seventeenth- and eighteenth-century French music.

In the original Paris edition of the *Principes du clavecin*, the twenty-eight chapters are followed by a section entitled 'Remarques sur quelques endroits de cet ouvrage' that are cued to specific places in the text. Since these Remarks are essentially footnotes expanding on certain points raised in the chapters, they have been treated as such in this translation and placed at the bottom of the relevant pages. They are distinguished from the translator's footnotes by the use of an asterisk instead of numbers.

In this edition, the musical examples reproduce those from the Ballard print. It was felt that the advantages of having access to the original notation of the examples outweighed the disadvantages of dealing with unfamiliar clefs in some of them. In a few places where there are examples of little pieces for both hands together, both the original and a transcription into modern clefs have been provided. Errors in the musical examples, of which there are a number, are noted in footnotes in the relevant places.

The original French chapter headings are also provided where appropriate, as are other French words or phrases at certain sensitive points of the translation. For those who wish to see St Lambert's original in its entirety, there is a facsimile of the Ballard edition available from Minkoff.

It is hoped that the three appendices will aid the reader's understanding of St Lambert's treatise by providing access to relevant materials that otherwise might not be readily at hand. The first appendix includes excerpts of pieces that St Lambert mentions, the second contains the ornament tables of the keyboard composers cited by St Lambert, and the third brings together all of St Lambert's ornament examples. The bibliography of seventeenth- and eighteenth-century sources includes a number of references to the works of composers of harpsichord music from St Lambert's period for those readers who would like to gain access to them.

I am very grateful to a number of people for their assistance with this project: to Albert Cohen, Richard Semmens, and Raoul Camus for providing me with necessary materials; and to Paul Gutlietti, David Fuller, Bruce Gustafson, and Peter Brown for useful conversation or correspondence on difficult points. I would like to thank Howard Mayer Brown and my editors at Cambridge University Press, Rosemary Dooley and Mandy Macdonald, for their meticulous attention to the preparation of the manuscript. I would also like to thank Prof. Neal Zaslaw of Cornell University whose support and guidance have been extremely helpful to me. I offer my heartfelt thanks to Prof. George Houle of Stanford University, without whose careful and caring assistance this project would not have been completed.

PRINCIPLES OF THE HARPSICHORD

Containing an exact explanation of all that concerns
Notation and the Keyboard.
With some Remarks necessary for the understanding
of several difficulties of music.
The whole divided into Chapters according to subject matter.
By Monsieur de SAINT LAMBERT

In Paris
At the house of Christophe Ballard, sole printer of the King for music
Rue St Jean de Beauvais, at Mont-Parnasse
1702
With License from His Majesty

Preface

Among all the instruments in use today, there is none, after the organ, as perfect as the harpsichord, since it combines several advantages not found all at the same time in any other instrument. It generally embraces the full range of the notes of music, of which the other instruments have but a share. It is well suited to playing all the voices at once and can always produce a perfect harmony. It stays in tune for a long time. It is extremely easy to play, not at all tiring for those who play it, and not requiring as do some other instruments a constrained posture which very often is not becoming to modest persons. This is what has given it such a sovereign position that all persons of distinction now want to learn how to play it.

This large number of persons who love the harpsichord made me think of presenting the public with a method book which would teach its principles, and I was even more inclined to do so when I saw that no other master had thought of it, although several had already written method books either for singing or for playing instruments. My primary concern in writing this one was to render it as clear and intelligible as it is true in its teachings. It seemed to me that a work of this nature would be useless if any obscurity prevailed within it, for an author should not expect that people will understand his little hints as he understands them himself, since he is filled with what he knows. He must realize that if he doesn't arrange his subject matter in an appropriate order and if he doesn't explain it simply, people will reap very little fruit from his labor. A man who writes a book to teach a science or an art must give himself the goal that the reader should be able to learn this science or art from his book without the aid of anyone else, assuming that these subjects are of a kind which can be so learned. And although music cannot be easily taught through writing, since that which relates to execution must almost of necessity be demonstrated orally or by hand, nevertheless books discussing music should be organized in such a way that theoretical concerns can be easily learned from them. An author who was negligent in this regard could scarcely be excused.

In order not to fall into this error, I have taken all the precautions that seemed necessary to me. I read my method book to people who had no acquaintance with music, in order to see if I had succeeded in my design of making myself understood to those who have no knowledge of this art. These people assured me in good faith and without flattering me that they easily understood all the principles that are taught in the book. After that I no longer feared to give this method book to the public, because I have such confidence in the people of whom I speak that I am persuaded that they would as little wish to deceive me as they are capable of deceiving themselves. Despite all that I do not flatter myself that I have made such a good method book that one could not perhaps find something to criticize. It is impossible for some little thing not to escape the attention even of the most capable people. Those whom I consulted, not having any knowledge of music, could simply see whether what I had written was intelligible, but not whether the reasoning behind my precepts was sound or whether I had forgotten some important point. This is why I beg those who are informed about these matters to excuse any mistakes I may have allowed to slip in, realizing that no one is infallible. But I would be still more deeply obliged to them if they would take the trouble to point out my errors directly to me. I would be extremely happy to defer to their wisdom and to correct my work on the basis of their opinions if a second edition should be made.

Foreword

For Those Who Want to Learn to Play the Harpsichord

Those who wish to learn to play the harpsichord must have two principal aptitudes in order to succeed. These two aptitudes are the *Ear* and the *Hand*.

The Ear consists of hearing the difference in the sounds of music and the different rhythms of airs with the greatest conceivable accuracy. Although at first this appears considerable, it is nevertheless certain that this extreme accuracy of the ear for intonation and rhythm is a gift granted to almost all men, like sight and speech. For there are few who do not sing and dance naturally, if not with all the delicacy and neatness which art has striven after, then at least with the correctness which it prescribes and which art itself has simply taken from nature. Therefore it is already an important point for those who wish to learn music or to play an instrument to know that they naturally have discernment of the ear, which is the first and foremost of all the aptitudes. But if they want to make sure of it further, let them take these tests that I will teach them. Let them see if when they listen to a piece of beautiful music they enter into all the movements which it tries to inspire; if they are deeply moved in the tender passages and aroused in the lively ones; if they sing internally that which they hear sung or played by others; if it seems to them that if only they had been shown how they could easily do the same. For if the thing appears easy to them, it is a sign that they will succeed in it, but if it seems surprising and difficult, they would do well to give it up. Let them then examine whether they have a taste for the melody and harmony of pieces; whether they enter into the rhythm of airs; whether they feel compelled to follow the beat despite themselves; whether they beat time without thinking about it, either with the head or otherwise. These are the true aptitudes which make the musician and without which one will uselessly strive to become one.

With regard to the aptitude of the Hand, there is no one who cannot have it, if he begins to practice early in life. This aptitude is nothing other than a great suppleness in the nerves which leaves the fingers free to move subtly. Childhood is the most appropriate time to acquire it. It has been well established that those who start in their youth become proficient and that those who only set about it late do not succeed. One cannot precisely assign an age when it is too late to start, because aptitudes vary depending on the individuals. Nevertheless, one may say to the advantage of the ladies that because of the natural delicacy of their sex, they have more aptitude in their hands at age thirty than do men at age fifteen or sixteen; but the most favorable period for both sexes is childhood, that is before ten years of age, and even from five or six.

Those who are endowed with these two aptitudes still have a task to give themselves: that is, to choose a good teacher. The success of a student's study depends as much on this choice as on all the rest. Someone who would have become proficient if he had been well taught has remained ignorant because his teacher was ignorant also; another person on the contrary has greatly advanced despite the fact that he had less aptitude, because his teacher knew how to get him to make good use of the little he had.

In order to be good, a teacher must have two qualities, knowledge and integrity, because two aptitudes are absolutely necessary in the teacher in order to produce a good student: that he should have both the ability and the desire to do so.

The knowledge of a teacher does not simply mean that he must be a skillful player of the harpsichord and an excellent composer of music; it must be understood that in addition to these two assets he should have the gift of demonstrating, which is a very distinct quality from that of being a famous musician.

A good teacher knows how to recognize in depth the different aptitudes of those who put themselves in his hands, and adapting himself to the grasp and capability of each one, he instructs each and every one in the manner which is best suited to the student. He creates as many different methods as he has different spirits to guide. He speaks as a child to children, reasonably to reasonable persons, and to both with intelligence and concision. He reveals his principles methodically and always presents them in the form of simple and isolated ideas. He doesn't encumber the memory of those whom he instructs with untimely distinctions. He teaches a general rule as if it were without exception, waiting for an occasion to produce this exception before speaking about it, because he knows that thus it is better understood, and that if he had discussed it at first, it would have hindered the impression of the general rule. He gives his first rule as if it were the only one he would ever have to talk about and when he passes to a second one, it is without making any mention of those which must follow.

Passing from theory to practice, a good teacher knows how to choose pieces for each of his students which are the most appropriate for the disposition of their hands. He even specially composes some for those who may need them. But after having placed some easy pieces in the hands of his students in order to entertain them at the beginning, he then gives them some which are directly opposed to the disposition of their hands in order to correct their failings.

A good teacher leads the student who has a great deal of ability far toward perfection and the one who has still more farther yet. He helps those students who have more aptitude than he does to play better than himself. But since he realizes that one cannot make progress without regular practice, he has his own secret for making the students enjoy learning. This talent is one of the most essential for teachers who have children to instruct, for the natural levity of young children often means that after having ardently wished to learn to play the harpsichord, they develop an aversion for it at the third or fourth lesson because of the difficulty it presents, and their dislike sometimes goes so far that an exercise which is called play and which really should be learned by playing is for them only the object of sadness and tears. Thus it is up to the teachers to find the means to relieve the tender pupils they are given of all the difficulties which discourage them and to act with them in such a manner that they devote themselves to their little exercises with pleasure, or at least with courage and perseverance.

After having spoken of the good qualities of the harpsichord teacher, it is necessary to say a few words about the failings he may have.

Leaving aside the dishonesty of not teaching conscientiously what one knows, a failing that I cannot imagine in any teacher at all, the only major defects I know of in a harpsichord teacher are those of not knowing how to place the hands of his pupils and of having them make an incorrect use of their fingers. The incorrect principles and false rules that he may teach are easy errors to correct when they are recognized, but the defect of using one's fingers badly is the most difficult to correct once it is acquired. It often lasts one's entire life as an eternal obstacle to the perfecting of one's playing. Since this defect only comes to us from our first teacher, it is important to choose one who knows how to avoid this mistake.

But this disadvantage is not to be feared by those who learn in Paris, where there are now such capable harpsichord teachers that I may confess without flattering them that they are the ones who have provided me with the image of the perfect teacher that I have depicted in this discourse.

Since the *agrément* called the *arpégé* is indicated in various ways in the works of the harpsichord masters, I decided to establish the use of the mark ⸲ in this method book as it is a better-known symbol and more likely to make an impression on the memory.[1]

The mark ⸴ was also chosen for the *pincé* as the one which has been used up to the present in all the method books of music.[2]

Apollo alone, or rather Nature
Makes the Poet, and the Musician.
Without her the spirit in vain gives itself torture;
One kills oneself and learns nothing.

1. See ch. XXVI, 'Concerning the *Arpégé*'. Cf. also St Lambert's comment in that chapter (p. 95) that he finds d'Anglebert's symbol preferable.
2. Despite this stated preference, St Lambert actually uses the symbol ⸴ only once in the *Principes*, when describing the *pincé* as done by Chambonnières and Lebègue. See ch. XXIII, 'Concerning the Pincé', p. 85. In the other examples of ornaments, and even more tellingly in his own two pieces at the end of the book, St Lambert uses d'Anglebert's symbol: ⸲'.

Principles of the Harpsichord

All the principles of the harpsichord may be reduced to the knowledge of two things, *notation* and the *keyboard*.

The *keyboard* is that assemblage of keys by means of which the harpsichord is made to sound.

Notation is the accumulation of the symbols or characters which are used to write music.

The keyboard is not difficult to understand; it is only necessary to know the name of each individual key.

Notation requires more diligence. In addition to the names of the symbols, it is necessary to know what they mean, and that is the subject of this treatise.

The principal symbols of notation are those which are called *notes*. These indicate the melody and the chords of the pieces and are, strictly speaking, the music itself. The others are less essential and only indicate the tempo of pieces, the *agréments* which must be performed, or some similar thing.

First I shall teach a knowledge of the notes, then I shall explain the keyboard, and speak of tempo, *agréments*, and the rest.

CHAPTER I

Concerning Notes and Clefs

(Des Notes et des Clefs)

Notes are symbols whose form is represented in the following example.

DEMONSTRATION OF THE NOTES

These notes are placed in different positions, on the [spaces and] parallel lines drawn one above the other.

Some people call these lines the musical *staff*.[1] The number of lines essential to the staff is fixed at five.* But other small lines are added on certain occasions according to the need one has of them for ascending or descending [above or below the staff], as may be seen in the example above.

The notes take their names from their positions relative to a certain symbol called a *clef* which is always marked at the beginning of the five essential lines. But before explaining how this is done, it must be said that there are three clefs in music, the C clef, the G clef, and the F clef,† represented in the following demonstration.

---

* The number is not the same in all tablatures. Those for the harpsichord, violin, viol, oboe, flute, and vocal music actually have only five essential lines. But the tablatures for theorbo and lute have six, and plainchant only four.

1. Fr. *échelle de la musique*. In ch. IX, 'Concerning the Voices', St Lambert deliberately changes from the use of this word to the more specific term *portée*, as he explains in a note to the reader. See ch. IX, p. 49.

† One usually says the clef of C sol ut, the clef of G re sol, the clef of F ut fa, in conformity to the gamut, which gives three names to each note, saying:

DEMONSTRATION OF THE CLEFS

One of these three clefs is always present at the beginning of the staff and it must be observed that although each of them is large enough to cover the entire width of the five lines, a clef is supposed to be placed on only one line, which is the one that passes through the middle of the clef. This may better be seen in the examples on the following pages.

It must also be observed that the clefs are not always placed on the same line but sometimes on one, and sometimes on another. However they are not indiscriminately placed on all the lines; each clef has its own assigned ones. The G clef is placed only on the first line, that is, the lowest of the five, or on the second, and never on the others; the F clef on the third or on the fourth and nowhere else, and the C clef on all the lines except the fifth which is the highest. A demonstration of this may be found in the following pages.

The names of the notes are C, D, E, F, G, A, B,[3] and it is the clef that indicates which note is called C, which D, which E, etc. It is done in this way:

☞ E si mi
D la re
C sol ut
B fa si
A mi la
G re sol
F ut fa

But as I have suppressed the gamut in this method book because it is no longer necessary since the mutations have been abolished, I will also suppress this way of naming the clefs, which is no more necessary than the gamut.[2]

2. St Lambert is referring to the hexachord system in use during the Middle Ages and Renaissance. In France the system of mutations was replaced by the present system (or 'system of Si' as St Lambert calls it in a Remark found later in this chapter, p. 15) in the middle of the 17th century. See Étienne Loulié, *Elements or Principles of Music*, trans. Albert Cohen (New York, 1965), pp. 43-4, first published in Paris in 1696, which discusses the transition from the old system to the new.

For the C Clef

When the C clef is the controlling one and is placed on the first line, that is on the lowest, one must say C on the first line. The order the notes have on the staff when ascending is the same as they have on the circle below, starting on any note and following the circle continuously to the right [i.e. clockwise] while always repeating the same names. When descending it is the same order as they have on the circle turning continuously to the left. Therefore it is easy to know the names of all the other notes once one knows where C is, because they are named relative to it.

For if one says C on the first line, D must be said on the step just above, that is between the first and second lines. Next E [must be said] on the second line, and F between the second and third, after that G on the third and so on for the rest, as is shown below.

When the C clef is placed on the second line, all the notes change their

3. The solmization syllables ut, re, mi, fa, sol, la, si found in St Lambert's text have been consistently replaced by the letter names of the notes in this translation.

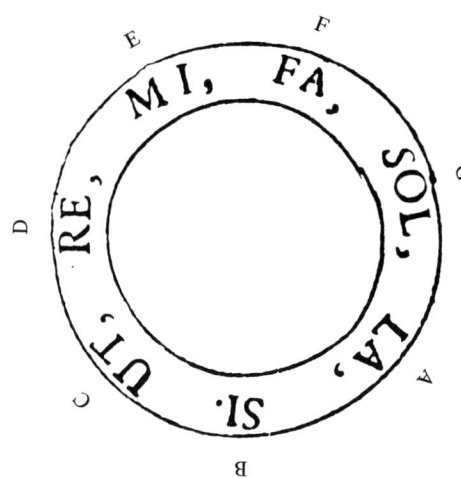

When the clef is on the fourth line, one says C on the fourth and then the names of the other notes in order.

For the G Clef

The G clef has the same effect as the C clef. When it is placed on the first line, it gives the line its name and one says G on it, A between the first and second lines, B on the second, and so on, following the order of the notes on the little circle given above.

If the clef is placed on the second line, it raises all the notes by two steps, and one says G on the second line, A between the second and third, B on the third, and the rest in order.

For the F Clef

Like the two others, the F clef gives its name to the line on which it is placed. When it is on the third line, one says F there, G between the third and fourth, A on the fourth, and the rest in the order of the circle.

If the clef is on the fourth line, then one says F there and the names of the other notes follow according to their order.

places: C must be said on the second line, D between the second and the third, E on the third, etc., as is explained in the demonstration below.

With the C clef placed on the third line, one says C on the third, D between the third and fourth, E on the fourth, etc., in order.

DEMONSTRATION OF ALL THE DIFFERENT POSITIONS OF THE CLEFS AND OF THE CHANGES IN NAME OF THE NOTES

The C Clef on the First Line [Soprano Clef]

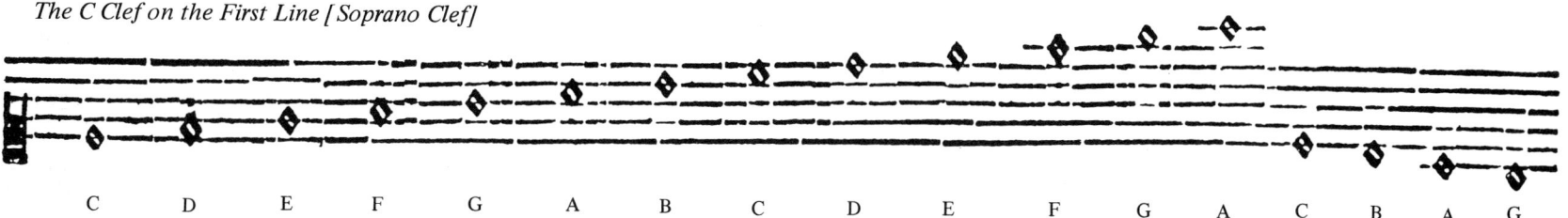

C D E F G A B C D E F G A C B A G

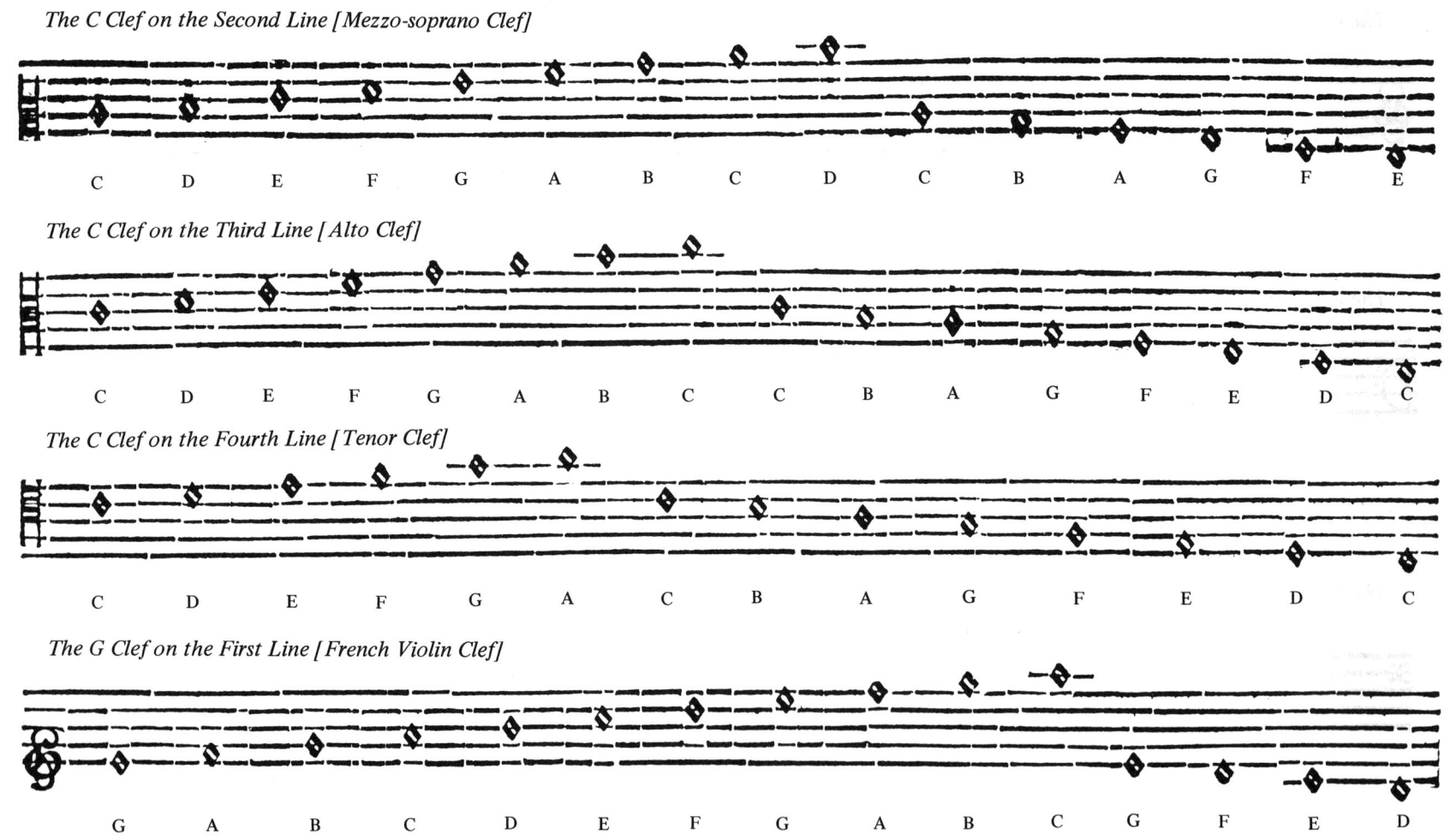

Notes and Clefs

The G Clef on the Second Line [Treble Clef]

The F Clef on the Third Line [Baritone Clef]

The F Clef on the Fourth Line [Bass Clef]

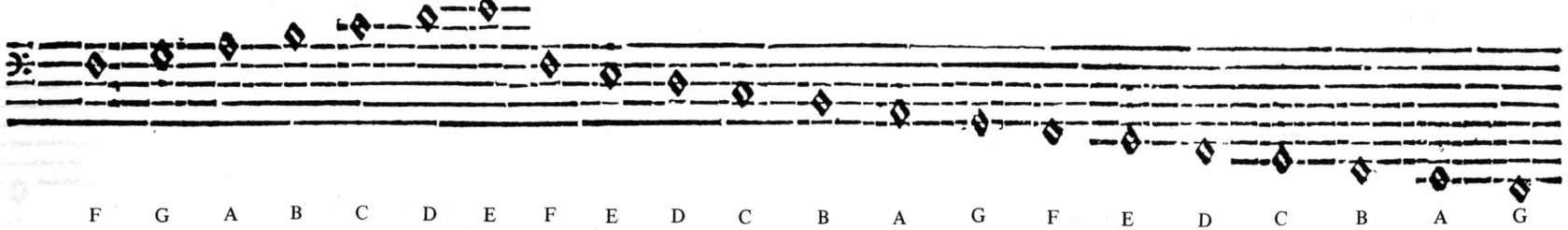

It is necessary to memorize the names of all the notes and to get them so well in one's head that when seeing written music one can read it immediately and say without hesitation, 'C G E F D A B G C D B C', etc. But in order to make this knowledge enter into one's memory in a methodical way, one must not attempt to learn all the clefs at once. At first one should study just a single clef, as for example the C clef placed on the first line, and when one knows the notes in this clef well, one may learn them for the same clef placed on the second line, then on the third, and finally the fourth. The same order should be observed for the other clefs. It is not necessary, however, to study the notes in all the different positions of each clef, unless one wants to know music in depth. For those who limit themselves to playing the harpsichord, it is sufficient to learn to name the notes in the clefs which are in use in harpsichord notation.

In harpsichord notation all three clefs are used, but each is placed on only one line: the C clef on the first line, the G clef on the second, and the F clef on the third.[4] Thus at first one may confine oneself to learning to name the notes in the clefs placed in these positions. But it is good to go on to the other positions later, because even on the harpsichord one is not always limited to those three and on certain occasions the C clef is placed on the third line, the F clef on the fourth, and the G clef on the first. This is why it is good to become familiar with all the different positions of the clefs, but it is sufficient at first to start with the three mentioned above.

This use of multiple and movable clefs is perhaps the most awkward aspect of harpsichord notation. See the Remarks, where it is proposed to abolish the use of multiple clefs and to make notation incomparably easier by reducing all the different ways of naming notes to one single, invariable way.*

---

4. Today these three clefs are called respectively the soprano, treble, and baritone clefs, and only the treble clef is in common use in keyboard music. In St Lambert's day, however, all three clefs (rarely the bass clef) were standard in harpsichord works. The two illustrative pieces he includes at the end of the *Principes* are written in the soprano and baritone and treble and baritone clefs respectively. The vast majority of the harpsichord works of d'Anglebert and Chambonnières use the same two clef combinations.

* It is certain that the multiplicity of clefs and the variation in their position is the most awkward thing about notation, above all for the harpsichord, and especially for beginners. Nothing tires them more than to see that they must name the notes one way in the upper voices and another way in the lower voices; that in the place where they say C in the right hand, they must say G in the left, etc. Beyond that, if the clef changes in the upper or lower part, as sometimes happens, their knowledge is overturned all of a sudden and they find themselves, so to speak, back at their ABCs. I have noticed that this is what slows pupils down the most in the progress of their studies and makes harpsichord pieces so difficult to play with the book open [i.e. at sight], even for those who are already advanced, and that other musicians have a much easier time of it because of the invariability of their clef. From this line of thought I imagined that it would be a badly needed reform for harpsichord notation to reduce it to the use of a single clef, as for the violin, which would be fixed on a single degree, in order to establish the naming of the notes in only one way for both the treble and the bass, or else still making use of the three clefs, to place them in such a way that the naming of the notes would be the same in all the voices. This reform would not be as considerable as it seems at first, because it would only be necessary to use the G clef on the first line for the treble parts and the F clef on the fourth line for the bass parts, as is done for the violin.[5] As for the alto and tenor voices, the C clef would be placed between the second and third lines, and to this end the clef's shape would be changed a little,[6] as I have done in the following example.

DEMONSTRATION OF A NEW WAY OF PLACING THE CLEFS IN HARPSICHORD NOTATION

G Clef: G A B C D E F G A B C

C Clef: G A B C D E F G A B C

F Clef: G A B C D E F G A B C

5. St Lambert means pieces written for solo violin and continuo. Today the G clef placed on the first line is usually called the French violin clef. It was used in France for other treble instruments as well. When the treble part is written in this clef and the bass in the bass clef, the notes have identical places on the staff but are two octaves apart.

6. St Lambert's usual C clef looks like this:
The shape of the one he proposes is different because it indicates that C is on a space rather than a line.

This way of placing the clefs would, as one may see here, make the naming of the notes the same in all the voices. This would be as much a relief to those who are learning to play the harpsichord as it would be correction of a major notational defect.

I didn't stop at the mere idea of this reform; I decided to try it out a few years ago. I had been called to the provinces to teach some persons of quality who wanted to have a master from Paris. Since I was given children who had no knowledge of music to instruct, I had the idea of giving them my new notation to test whether or not they would learn faster from it, and I had the pleasure of seeing that it gave them an extreme facility and that at the end of only three lessons on learning the notes, a little girl of five was ready to study by herself the pieces that I had given her, and that persons of a more advanced age could do it starting with the first lesson.

After all, I am not so favorably disposed toward my new system that I can't see that it has a considerable drawback, that is its very novelty. I realize that since it has not been received and established everywhere, someone who knew no other system would know nothing, since he would be unable to learn any of the pieces that are written with the ordinary system.

But if it were finally established, the defect of its novelty would last but a short while and with the other system being gradually abolished, this one would soon remain alone by virtue of being the most convenient. The system of Si, reasonable as it is, had this same defect of novelty at the beginning, but since it is infinitely better than the system of mutation, it had no trouble in establishing its supremacy.[7] Mine being no less useful to the harpsichord than the

7. St Lambert is referring to the change from the hexachord system to the modern system of fixed ut or do. See note 2 above.

The System That Must be Used in Order to Learn to Name the Notes

In order to imprint the notes on the memory, it is first necessary to remember the names of the ones on the lines. For example, if someone wants to learn to name the notes in the C clef placed on the first line, he must remember that one says C on this line, E on the second, G on the third, B on the fourth, and D on the fifth.

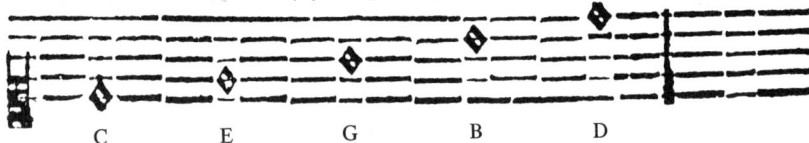

☞ system of Si is to music in general, I could have reason to hope that it will enjoy the same success. However, I am not counting on it, given the nature of public opinion. What is certain is that I don't presume to dictate to anyone; I only propose what I think can improve the art that I profess. If the masters judge that I am mistaken, let them challenge me; I willingly submit myself to their judgment and will not be more mortified to find them opposed to my feelings than I would glorify myself for having won them all over to my side.[8]

    8. St Lambert's notational innovation did not catch on. The four books of harpsichord pieces published by François Couperin between 1713 and 1730 use six different clefs with frequent changes between them. Jean-Philippe Rameau's *Pièces de clavecin* of 1724 also use a variety of clefs, although the modern combination of treble and bass clefs is quite frequent. Similar notational reforms were proposed by other 18th-century theorists, notably Michel Pignolet de Montéclair and Abbé La Cassagne, with equal success (see Translator's Introduction).

He must get used to this and be able to say when ascending, 'CEGBD', and when descending, 'DBGEC', with the same facility. In order for this person to see if he really knows them, he must test himself by taking a sheet or book of music and trying to say correctly and right away: 'This note is a G, that one an E, this other one a B', etc.

When he no longer hesitates in naming the notes on the lines, he must learn with the same method those that are in the spaces, that is between the lines.

After that he must learn the notes which are above the five essential lines, using the same system:

and finally those which are below.

One must not study the notes in the G clef before knowing them perfectly in the C clef, for haste in studying makes one regress rather than advance. It is necessary to be sure of the first thing before passing on to the second, to consider always only one thing at a time, and to give oneself the simplest and clearest idea of it possible; and this is true for all kinds of study. When one knows the notes in the G clef as well as those in the C clef, one may learn them in the F clef. It doesn't matter, however, with which of the three one begins, for it is necessary to know them all equally well, but one should remember to study only one clef at a time, and while learning to use the system that I have taught here.

CHAPTER II

Concerning the Keyboard

(Du Clavier)

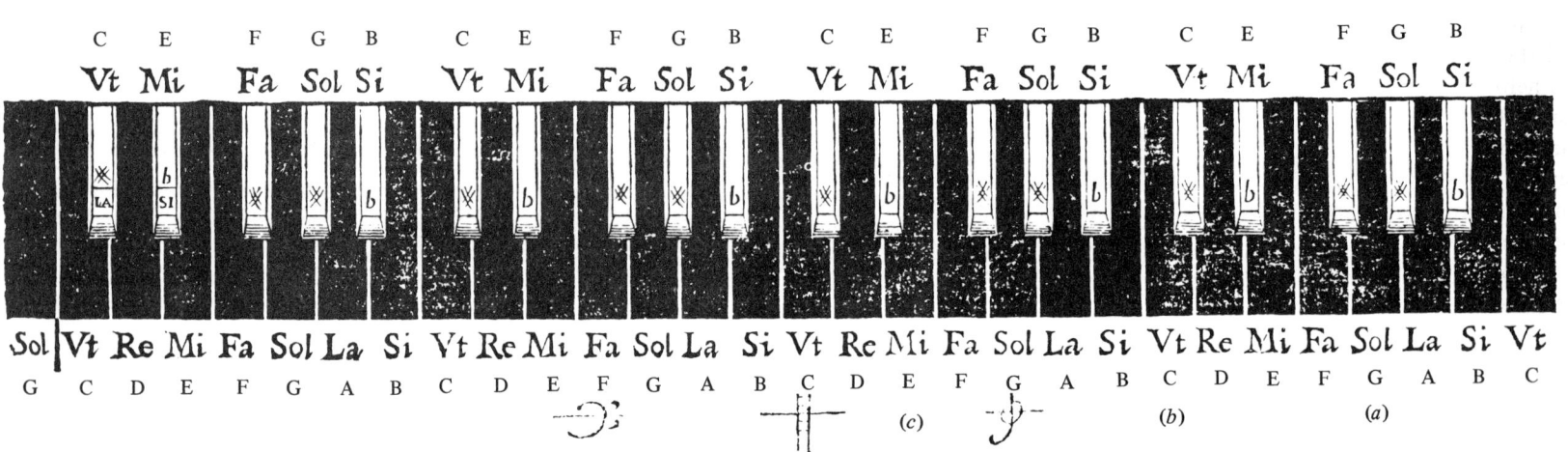

A knowledge of the keyboard must naturally follow that of the notes, since it is on the keyboard that pieces are executed.

It seemed to me that the best way to teach the keyboard was to have an entire one drawn here, on which the name of each key was written in order. The keyboard is composed of two types of keys, black and white.[1]

---

1. On the French harpsichords of St Lambert's time, the color of the keys is the reverse of the piano keyboard: the naturals are black and the accidentals white.

The names of the black keys are, like the notes, C D E F G A B, repeated several times.

The white keys have the same names as the black keys and are further distinguished by the marks I have put on them, which I will discuss elsewhere. For the moment, it is sufficient to say that among the white keys the C, F, and G keys are characterized by the mark ♯, and the two keys B and E by the mark ♭. Among the white keys there is no D or A.[2] (See the Remarks, but first see Chapter XVI, 'Concerning the Flat'.[3])

Some people call the white keys in general *accidentals*.

The white keys are distributed by twos and threes, and this distribution serves to make the keys recognizable to the eye, the black keys as well as the white, for without this different division everything would be confused and the eye would distinguish nothing. Therefore in order to make use of the help provided by this arrangement, it must be said that the black key named C is the one on the left of the two white keys, that D is between the two, and that E is on their right. F is on the left of the three white keys, G between the first and second, A between the second and third, and finally B is on the right of the same three white keys. Once one knows these seven black and five white keys, one knows the entire keyboard.

Among the black keys there are three which correspond to clefs: the F clef, the C clef, and the G clef, as in the notation (see the Remarks concerning the names of the clefs*). These are the keys next to which I marked the clef symbols in the drawing of the keyboard.

The first black key and the first two white keys [on the lower end of the keyboard] do not have the names which they naturally should have, because it has been found to be more suitable to tune them to pitches other than those prescribed for them, for the advantage of the bass line. Concerning this, it must be said that there are some instruments that lack this first black key, which is a G, and whose keyboard thus starts with C. There are others whose first white key or even the first two are double [i.e. split] and make two pitches. The two names on each of these keys [on the drawing of the keyboard] are the names they have when they are double. When they are single, the first is usually called A, the second B.[4]

---

* I name the clefs in this order because it is the one they have among the keys of the harpsichord. The first time I spoke of them I named the C clef before the others since it is with C that we begin to count the notes.

4. St Lambert is describing what is now called the short octave, which is a means of extending the range of an instrument downward without adding more keys. Thus a harpsichord whose bottom note appears to be BB is actually tuned as follows: BB is tuned to GG, C♯ to AA, and E♭ to BB, thereby providing a diatonic stepwise bass line down to GG. Sometimes the lowest two white keys are split and each given two sets of strings, in which case the front parts of the keys are set at the more frequently used pitches AA and BB, while the back parts are set at C♯ and E♭, as indicated in St Lambert's drawing of the keyboard. At the other end, the keyboard extends upward to the C two octaves above middle C. St Lambert's information is an important piece of evidence in establishing the normal range of late 17th-century French harpsichords, for there are very few surviving instruments from the period. Frank Hubbard, in *Three Centuries of Harpsichord Making* (Cambridge, Mass., 1965), pp. 100–5, discusses four surviving 17th-century French harpsichords, all of which have two manuals. Three of them have the range St Lambert describes, of GG/BB to c′′′ with a short octave, and one has a split key arrangement. The fourth instrument is fully chromatic from GG to c′′′; however, it is unsigned and undated and may be later. A photograph of the Tibaut harpsichord (1679), one of the four discussed by Hubbard,

---

2. The distinction St Lambert makes between the notes that are sharps and those that are flats is due to the use of unequal temperaments in the tuning of keyboard instruments prevalent at that time. See ch. XVI, note 2, p. 62.

3. The passage in the Remarks discussing this subject is actually part of a Remark concerning the sharp, flat, and natural belonging to ch. XVII (pp. 64ff). The discussion of the lack of D and A among the white keys of the harpsichord may be found in the last two paragraphs of the subheading 'On the Flat', pp. 65-6.

But one need not burden oneself with the names of these two keys because they are used quite rarely, especially in pieces learned in the beginning, and before the time comes to use them, there will be plenty of opportunity to find out from someone what the names of the keys are on one's own harpsichord or spinet,[5] for they are not the same on all instruments, and the difference depends on the method of the tuner. But ordinarily they are set at A and B.

It is not necessary to say that with harpsichords which have two keyboards, both are completely alike, in the names of the notes, in appearance, in everything. This is self-evident.[6]

One must become as secure in the knowledge of the keys on the keyboard as in the knowledge of the notes in the notation, and to be able to say with equal facility, that is, immediately and without hesitation, 'This key is named G, that C, and this other E', etc.

---

may be seen in Raymond Russell, *The Harpsichord and Clavichord* (New York, 1973), plate 43, clearly showing the two split keys in each manual, as well as the black naturals and white accidentals.

5. The spinet of St Lambert's time was a single-manual instrument with the same mechanism as the harpsichord but much smaller, approximately three feet long instead of six to seven feet. The 17th-century French spinets discussed by both Russell (pp. 54-5) and Hubbard (pp. 104-5) have the same GG-c''' range with the short octave as the harpsichords of the period, although some spinets were tuned an octave higher. A photograph of a late 17th-century French spinet may be seen in Russell, plate 44.

6. It is not quite as self-evident as St Lambert would have it, given that Flemish double harpsichords from the late 16th and early 17th centuries, which were undoubtedly to be found in France at the time, used the second manual for purposes of transposition. See Hubbard, pp. 63ff. St Lambert also neglects to mention the difference in timbre between the two manuals.

CHAPTER III

Concerning the Manner of Studying Pieces
(De la Manière d'Étudier les Pièces)

Once one knows the notes and the keyboard perfectly, it merely remains to take a book of harpsichord pieces, to put it before one's eyes, to read the notes written there, and to play them on the keyboard as one reads them. The harpsichord will sing the airs that are written in the book, provided that one observes everything I say in the following pages. This is in general how to study pieces, but to be more specific I will first remark that it is on the black keys that one plays, not on the whites, which are used only on certain occasions that I will mention later.

The notes must be played at specific places on the keyboard relative to their positions on the paper. This will be better explained by some examples.

The note seen here is a G, thus to express it one must play a G on the keyboard. But since there are several Gs, one may not know which to choose. The clef removes this difficulty.

First of all, the notes must be played on the keyboard within the context of the clef which is indicated on the paper. Second, it is necessary to play them closer to or farther from the key which corresponds to the clef, depending on whether they are closer to or farther from the scale-degree, or rather the line, on which the clef is located. Thus for the note given here, first it must be considered that it is the G clef which is in effect, then that this note is sitting directly on the scale-degree of the clef. These two circumstances mean that to express this note, it is necessary to play precisely that key on the keyboard which corresponds to the G clef.

For this note, which is also a G and is not on the scale-degree of the clef but seven steps higher, it is necessary to play the G at the upper end of the keyboard (at (*a*), in the drawing of the keyboard, p. 18 above), seven keys above the one corresponding to the G clef. The right side of the keyboard is called the high side and the left side the low, because in going from left to right the pitches get higher, and the other way around, going from right to left, they get lower.

This note, a C, must be played between the two Gs I just mentioned, because it occupies that level on the paper (see (*b*), on the drawing of the keyboard).

This note, an E, must be played two keys lower than [the note corresponding to] the G clef, because on the paper it is two steps lower than the pitch of the clef (see (*c*), on the drawing of the keyboard).

I don't believe it necessary to speak any further about this rule. It is one of the simplest in the book and should be understandable to people who have even the slightest aptitude.

The same thing is to be observed in regard to the other clefs.

CHAPTER IV

Concerning Note Values

(De la Valeur des Notes)

It is not sufficient to know where the notes must be played on the keyboard; it is also necessary to know how long to hold each one after having played it, for every note has a specific length which must be neither shortened nor lengthened. This is what is called observing the value of the notes. Some must go by very quickly, others proceed more soberly, and still others very slowly. The difference in their length is determined by their shape. There are five kinds of notes, whose names and shapes are indicated here.

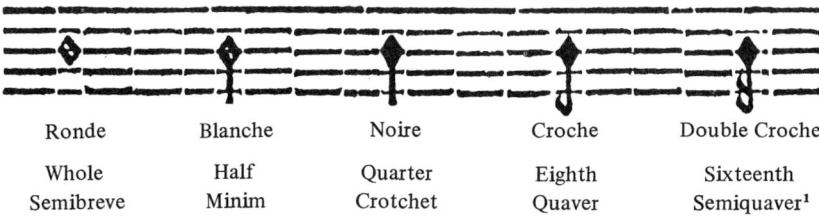

Ronde	Blanche	Noire	Croche	Double Croche
Whole	Half	Quarter	Eighth	Sixteenth
Semibreve	Minim	Crotchet	Quaver	Semiquaver[1]

1. Hereafter American terminology for the note values will be used.

The whole note is worth the most of all these notes, that is to say it is the note which must move the slowest. After that comes the half note, and then the others according to the order in which I have arranged them.

The whole note is worth
$$\begin{cases} 2 \text{ half notes} \\ 4 \text{ quarter notes} \\ 8 \text{ eighth notes} \\ 16 \text{ sixteenth notes} \end{cases}$$

The half note is worth
$$\begin{cases} 2 \text{ quarter notes} \\ 4 \text{ eighth notes} \\ 8 \text{ sixteenth notes} \end{cases}$$

The quarter note is worth
$$\begin{cases} 2 \text{ eighth notes} \\ 4 \text{ sixteenth notes} \end{cases}$$

The eighth note is worth 2 sixteenth notes

The sixteenth note is the smallest of the note values.[2]

2. This statement is modified in the Remark in ch. V, p. 26, where St Lambert says that composers occasionally use thirty-second notes.

The value of a note is expressed, as I said, by the length of time it is held after it has been played. Thus it is necessary to stay longer on those notes worth the most and to release earlier those worth the least. One must hold a whole note for as long as is necessary to express sixteen sixteenths, because a whole note is worth sixteen sixteenths. I compare a whole note to an enormous giant who in a single step can advance as far as a dwarf could in sixteen steps. If two men of such different height were walking together, it would be necessary for the dwarf to run with all his might while the giant would merely be strolling. This comparison is all the more appropriate to music in that there are notes which run very quickly while others walk slowly, and still others proceed at a moderate speed, all nevertheless reaching for the same goal, that is the end of the piece, at the same time. Thus, in order to know how much time must be given to each individual note value, it is sufficient to know how much must be given to a single one, since all the notes are regulated in proportion to each other.

The quarter note, which is in the middle of the note values, is the one by which all the others are determined. Thus it is only necessary to say how to regulate the quarter note, but here I admit that I find myself in an awkward position. It is not easy to express in words the length of time that must be devoted to a quarter note, seeing as that amount of time is so small that its measurement cannot be found either in a day, an hour, or even in the smallest part of a minute, for the length of the quarter note is less than all that. Let us then seek an example which may serve to measure time in smaller units and which measures it equally. Perhaps the pendulum of a clock could help us, for it describes fairly regular and fairly frequent movements, but it is not well enough suited to the task since there are clocks of all sizes whose pendulum movements are therefore different, so it is not easy to determine which clock to go by. I can see nothing more apt than the steps a man takes while walking. His steps are all very regular unless he is lame. We will thus make use of them and say that the quarter notes in a piece must be regulated by the steps of a man who walks rather quickly and who could cover one and a quarter leagues in an hour. Each quarter note must last as long as it takes him to take one step.[3] Thus it is very important to get into one's head the idea of this little unit of time in order to use it to regulate the notes of the pieces one plays. The best way to fix it in one's head is without a doubt to go walking oneself at the speed I just mentioned, and to pay close attention to feeling the divisions of time made by the steps while walking in this way and especially to the equality of these divisions. If this equality is not perceptible, one will never regulate the notes correctly. I will call this little unit of time which is used to take a step a beat, according to the terminology of musicians, and this term which belongs to the art I discuss in this book will help me make myself understood.

I will thus say that a quarter note must last for one beat, that a half note lasts for two, and a whole note four. Since an eighth note is equal to only half of a quarter note, two of them must go by within the duration of one beat, and when there are sixteenth notes, there are four per beat. This is how one adjusts the notes in relation to their value, and it is in observing this rule that pieces are given that movement which is the soul of music.

Before leaving this chapter it would be appropriate to call the attention of the reader to the fact that eighth and sixteenth notes do not always have the shape that I gave them on the preceding page [p. 23], and that they are only made that way when they appear singly as they do in that

---

3. See ch. VIII, where St Lambert discusses a system of proportionality of tempo as indicated by the time signature and based on this walking speed. Given his obviously strong desire to find a good method for indicating tempo, it is surprising that St Lambert was unaware of Étienne Loulié's chronometer, a metronome-like device based on a pendulum of variable length designed specifically for the purpose of providing accurate tempo indications, which was written up by Loulié six years before St Lambert's book and published by Christophe Ballard, also St Lambert's publisher. See Loulié, *Elements*, pp. 84-90.

place. But when there are several in a row, the eighth notes are attached together by a single pen stroke, and the sixteenth notes by a double stroke.

Sometimes they are also separated in the following way.*

The other notes are never drawn other than in the way I have represented them, but it may further be observed that for the notes which have stems, the stems may be turned either up or down without making any difference.

* There are some people who claim that these two different ways of drawing eighth notes establish a difference in the way of executing them; that when they are attached together by the line that makes them eighth notes, they must be played unequally, and when they are separated and each given a separate hook, they must on the contrary be played equally. But this is a rule to which one should not pay any attention, for it is not the shape of the eighth notes that determines how they should be played, but rather the time signature at the beginning of the piece, the name and character of the piece, and above all the good taste of the player.[4]

4. St Lambert's disclaimer notwithstanding, there are pieces from the period in which the separate stemming of eighth notes does seem to indicate their equal performance, particularly in C or ¢ as indicators that the inequality should occur on the sixteenth note. See, for example, the allemande 'La Loureuse' by Chambonnières, or the second fugue in ¢ in A. Raison's 'La Paix tant désirée', in his *Second livre d'orgue*. However, St Lambert is correct in warning that one should not rely on this method alone when determining the appropriate performance of eighth notes; there are other important criteria including the ones he mentions here. This warning is particularly appropriate today in light of the fact that modern editions frequently alter the original stemming of the notes. Cf. St Lambert's later comments about inequality, p. 46.

CHAPTER V

Concerning the Dot

(Du Point)

In music the use of the dot is to increase notes by half of their natural value, and to this end it is placed after the note to be increased.

These notes, whose value is increased by half by the dot, are called dotted notes. Thus one speaks of a dotted whole note, a dotted half note, a dotted quarter note, and a dotted eighth note. The sixteenth note is never dotted.*

A dotted whole note is worth	3 half notes / 6 quarter notes / 12 eighth notes / 24 sixteenth notes
A dotted half note is worth	3 quarter notes / 6 eighth notes / 12 sixteenth notes
A dotted quarter note is worth	3 eighth notes / 6 sixteenth notes
A dotted eighth note is worth	3 sixteenth notes

When a whole note is dotted, it must last for six of the beats I discussed instead of four, because it is increased by half. The dotted half note must last three beats, the others in proportion, which I will explain more specifically in the chapter concerning meter [ch. VIII].

* According to the rules, the sixteenth note is never dotted, since being the smallest of the note values it can naturally not be divided. This does not prevent it from being found dotted as are the others, in certain types of music, because there are some composers who, in order to indicate very fast passages, use thirty-second notes, and since a thirty-second note (when one wishes to use it) is worth half as much as a sixteenth note, then the sixteenth note may be dotted, being no

☞ longer the smallest of the note values. But this is rare and is only done as a liberty.

CHAPTER VI

Concerning the Tie

(De la Tenue)

The notes whose values are not increased by a dot could well be called simple note values, and those which are increased by a dot compound note values, since each note has its own specific value which is determined by its shape, and if this value is increased by a dot, it creates a compounding of the value.

But there is another way to compound the value, by means of a symbol called the tie, which varies the natural value of the notes even more than the dot does. For the dot only increases the value of a note by half, and the tie increases it sometimes by double its value, sometimes by triple, sometimes by half, sometimes by a fourth, and sometimes by an eighth. Thus by means of the tie, notes can be made of whatever value one wishes, and it was for this purpose that the tie was invented.*

---

* The beauty of the melody sometimes requires that a note be held for a long time or for a certain length of time to which no single note value corresponds. In this case one uses the tie and by means of it composes the desired note-length, which by greatly varying the note values, adds a great deal to the charm of the melody.

The tie is so named because it serves to attach several notes together and from all these notes to make only one. The sign for it may be seen in the following example. It is placed between the notes which it joins, as this example shows.

DEMONSTRATION OF THE TIE AND ITS USE

The notes that the tie joins together are never placed on different pitches; that is, it doesn't join a C to a D or an E, nor an F to an A or a B, but it always joins a C to a C on the same degree, or a G to the same G, etc., as the example above shows.

If the tie connects only two notes, it is only notated once (as at A, in the example below). If it connects three notes, it is notated twice (as at B). If it connects four notes, it is notated three times (as at C), etc.

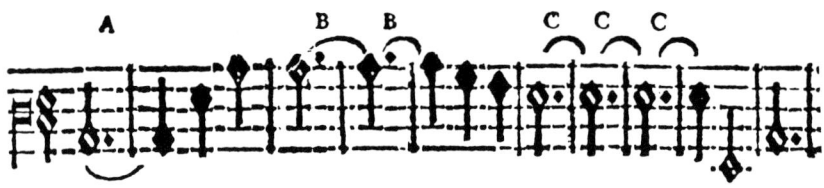

Several notes joined together by one or several ties should be considered as only one note to which is given the value of all the notes taken together. Thus two quarter notes joined together must be regarded as a half note, four quarters as a whole note, two eighths as a quarter note, etc.

The way of expressing these notes is to play them as if there were only one. Thus it is necessary to give the first note the value of all those connected to it and not to play the others. In other words, after having played the first of the tied notes, one must not lift the finger to play the others, but rather keep holding the first note until the time it would have taken to play all the others has ended.

CHAPTER VII

Concerning the Slur

(De la Liaison)

The slur greatly resembles the tie in its symbol and use. Like the tie, it connects several notes together, and thus increases their value, but with the difference that the tie only joins notes on the same pitch, while the slur only joins notes placed on different pitches, as may be seen in the following example.

DEMONSTRATION OF THE SLUR AND ITS USE

Of the several notes connected by a tie, only the first is played and then held for as long as it would take to play all the others, as we said in the preceding chapter. However, it is not the same with the slur.

All the notes that the slur encloses are played, and the effect of the slur is that all these notes are held after having been played, even if their value has expired, and they are only released when it is time to release the last note.

In order to explain this more clearly, let us imagine four notes connected by a slur and marked ABCD according to the order in which they are arranged (see the example above). A must be played first, B second, C third, and D fourth, but in playing B, A must not be released, nor in playing C must A or B be released, nor in playing D must A, B, or C be released. They must all be held and not released until it is time to release the last one, that is, when D has reached its full value. Then they are all released simultaneously even though they were struck one after the other.[1]

1. This particular use of the slur must be understood in light of St Lambert's comment at the end of the chapter that the slur is used almost exclusively in preludes, by which he means the unmeasured prelude as found in the works of 17th-century composers such as d'Anglebert, Lebègue, and Louis Couperin. Nicolas Lebègue confirms the applicability of this meaning of the slur to his own preludes in a letter replying to an Englishman who had written to him for information: 'The little circle [i.e. the slur] which begins at the note below, and continoues to a notte above (in the same line) doth signifie that ye must hold out all the nottes enclosed by that cercle without quyting any of them after ye have touched them and that for preserving the harmonie' (Bruce Gustafson, 'A letter from Mr Lebègue concerning

To complete the comparison between the tie and the slur, it may be observed that the tie is notated more than once when it connects more than two notes, as we said before, but that the slur is only notated once, whether it connects three, four, or more notes.

The general rule is to hold down all the notes enclosed by the slur until it is time to release the last one, but there are some instances when they must not all be held. When the first and last notes are long, that is whole or half notes, and the others are short, that is eighth or sixteenth notes, as in the following example, only the first and last notes are held and all the others are released.

But even without looking to see if the first and last notes are longer than the others, it is enough that the notes enclosed by the slur move by step to make it obligatory to hold only the first and the last. Thus in the following examples, even though the notes all have the same value, only the first and last of those enclosed by the slur should be held, because they move by step and not disjunctly.

his preludes', *Recherches*, 1977, p. 10). An example of a prelude by Nicolas Lebègue which illustrates this use of the slur may be found in appendix A.

In the ornament table appended to his *Pièces de clavecin* of 1724, Rameau also gives the same meaning to the slur.

Some other times, even though the notes enclosed by the slur move disjunctly, one still releases the notes in the middle, holding only the first and the last, and this is when the slur is turned in a certain way which seems to exclude the notes in the middle and to join only those which begin and end the passage. An example will explain this better.

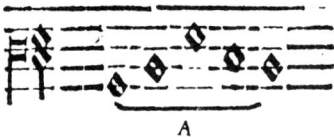

Of the five notes seen here accompanied by slur A, only the first and last are to be held, because it is apparent that it only joins the first note to the last one, since the slur is turned in the way it is. But if it were turned in this other way (see example B), it would be necessary to hold all the notes.[2]

2. It is difficult to know exactly what distinguishes these two examples from each other in St Lambert's mind. The phrase in French 'lorsque la liaison est tournée d'un certain sens', translated here as 'when the slur is turned in a certain way', could have a number of meanings. It could indicate which direction the slur is facing, and in example A the slur is under the notes and turned upwards, whereas in example B it is above and facing down. However, in his earlier examples of the use of the slur, St Lambert uses slurs placed above or below the notes without distinction between them. Nor does there appear to be a difference between those that are more rounded ⌒ and those that are squared ⊓. The French word *tourner* can also mean simply to express or present, which makes the range of possible interpretations even wider. Slur A is drawn closer to the notes, thus perhaps pointing more directly to the first and last notes than slur B, which is farther away from them and seems more to enclose

The slur is particularly used in preludes and sometimes in other pieces, but less frequently.[3]

Among the Remarks is one concerning the slur, but it is not directed to beginners.*

* *Remark concerning the slur*: In my opinion not enough use is made of the slur. It is used almost exclusively in preludes and it should, it seems to me, be used in all pieces in the places where the voices enter one after the other. For on this type of occasion, rests are placed on the empty beats of the measure for the regularity of the composition, and in order to indicate the joining of one voice to another, superfluous notes are added which are attached by ties to the first notes, and all this creates confusion in the score that is very awkward for the players. The slur would unravel this confusion if it were used in place

☞ of these double notes and useless rests. For example, if instead of indicating a measure in which the voices enter one after the other in this way:

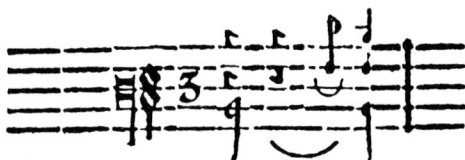

it were indicated in this way:

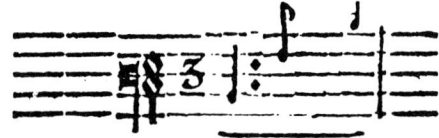

the effect on execution of the measure would be the same. By making the notation clearer and simpler, this second way would make it much easier [to read], although less regular for those who want to do things strictly.

them all. It is also possible that the printer simply made a mistake and failed to distinguish adequately between the two examples. There are enough printing errors in the musical examples elsewhere in this book to make this last hypothesis not unreasonable.

3. See ch. XXIV, 'Concerning the *Port de Voix*', for a different use of the slur.

CHAPTER VIII

Concerning the Signs that Indicate Meter and Tempo

(Des Signes qui Marquent la Mesure et le Mouvement[1])

At the beginning of a piece, right after the first clef there is always a certain symbol called the time signature, which is placed in every piece in order to indicate its character. Most often the time signature is made up of one or more numbers[2] and sometimes also a letter or something similar.[3] But before speaking of time signatures, two things must be brought to the attention of the reader. First, in all pieces the notes are separated into small equal units called *measures*. This does not mean that every measure in a piece has an equal number of notes, but rather that the notes of one measure taken together are equal in value to the notes of another measure also taken together, just as a crown is equal either to two pieces of thirty *sous* or to four pieces of fifteen *sous*. Thus the notes are separated in order to mark the divisions which occur naturally in the melody, for the melody of a piece is not composed without order and reason; it is made up of several little units which each have a complete meaning. A piece of music somewhat resembles a piece of rhetoric [*une Pièce d'Éloquence*], or rather it is the piece of rhetoric which resembles the piece of music, since harmony, number, measure, and the other similar things which a skillful orator observes in the composition of his works belong more naturally to music than to rhetoric [*la Rhétorique*]. In any case, just as a piece of rhetoric is a whole unit which is most often made up of several parts [*parties*], each of which is composed of sentences [*périodes*], each having a complete meaning, these sentences being composed of phrases [*membres*], the phrases of words [*mots*], and the words of letters, so the melody of a piece of music is a whole unit which is always composed of several sections [*reprises*]. Each section is composed of cadences [*cadences*][4] which have a complete meaning and are the sentences of the

---

1. The three important words in this heading can only be imperfectly translated into English, particularly because the concepts behind them have changed since 1702. The time signature [*signe*] did not merely tell how many beats there are in a measure, but indicated, as St Lambert says in the first sentence of this chapter, the character of the piece. It also gave some indication of its *mouvement*, that is its tempo, as well as its movement in the larger sense. The word *mesure* is particularly elusive. It usually means either meter or a measure of music, or the two simultaneously, but it can also imply a sense of measure and proportion. It has generally been translated here as either 'meter' or 'measure', but the reader should bear in mind its combined meaning.
2. E.g. 2 or ¾.
3. E.g. C or ¢.

4. St Lambert presumably means a long phrase concluding with a cadence.

melody. The cadences are often composed of phrases [*membres*], the phrases of measures [*mesures*], and the measures of notes. Thus the notes correspond to the letters, the measures to words, the cadences to sentences, the sections to parts, and the whole to the whole. But these divisions in the melody are not perceived by all those who hear music sung or played on some instrument. One must be trained in music in order to be aware of them, except for some which are so glaring that everyone understands them. However, these divisions are marked in the notation by the bars which separate the measures and by some other characteristics which I will discuss in their place.

The second thing to observe is that in order to give oneself a more tangible idea of the duration that must be given to each note in a piece, musicians have invented [a system] of making certain equal movements of the hand by means of which they regulate their notes. This is what is called beating time [*battre la mesure*], and this term is used for two reasons: first, because these movements must be perceptibly marked as if one were beating on something, which is explained more thoroughly elsewhere [pp. 38-9]; and second, because they are set at a specific number for every individual measure in order to regulate each like the others and are repeated as many times as there are measures in the piece. There are some pieces in which one must make four hand movements for each measure, others where one makes three, and others which only require two. These movements are called *beats* [*temps*], and when one makes four per measure it is called beating quadruple time. If one makes only three movements it is called beating triple time and if only two, it is called beating duple time.

Thus the time signature placed at the beginning of a piece indicates three things at once: how many notes there must be in each measure;[5]

---

5. I.e. how many equal notes or their equivalent must be in each measure, as St Lambert explained at the beginning of the chapter.

how many counts per measure to beat; and what tempo, that is, what speed or what gravity must be given to the piece.

There are nine different time signatures, each of which has its own particular significance, and whose names and symbols are given below.[6]

NAMES AND DEMONSTRATION OF THE TIME SIGNATURES

C	₵	2	$\frac{4}{8}$
Major	Minor	Binary	Four-Eight

$\frac{3}{2}$	3	$\frac{3}{8}$
Three-Two, or Double Triple	Ternary, or Simple Triple	Three-Eight

$\frac{6}{4}$		$\frac{6}{8}$
Six-Four		Six-Eight

We will first tell how many notes per measure each time signature requires, then we will speak of beats and of tempo.

The major time signature is worth four quarter notes per measure or the equivalent of four quarter notes.

---

6. Note the absence of the time signatures $\frac{2}{4}$ and $\frac{3}{4}$, which were not found in 17th-century French music but were common to Italian music and, in the early 18th century, to Italianate music in France. $\frac{2}{4}$ and $\frac{3}{4}$, being foreign imports, have completely different implications for tempo and character than do the native 2 and 3. The performer should be aware that some 20th-century editions of 17th- and 18th-century music have modernized and thereby falsified the time signatures.

The minor time signature is also worth four quarter notes or their equivalent.

The binary time signature is once again worth four quarter notes or their equivalent.

The time signature $\frac{4}{8}$ is worth four eighth notes or their equivalent instead of four quarter notes.

The time signature $\frac{3}{2}$ or double triple is worth three half notes or their equivalent.

The ternary time signature or simple triple is worth three quarter notes or their equivalent.

The time signature $\frac{3}{8}$ is worth three eighth notes or their equivalent.

The time signature $\frac{6}{4}$ is worth six quarter notes or their equivalent.

The time signature $\frac{6}{8}$ is worth six eighth notes or their equivalent.

EXAMPLE, OR DEMONSTRATION OF EVERYTHING JUST SAID CONCERNING TIME SIGNATURES

Major Time Signature

Minor Time Signature

Binary Time Signature

Four-Eight Time Signature

Three-Two Time Signature

Ternary Time Signature

Three-Eight Time Signature

Six-Four Time Signature

There is a small remark to make regarding this time signature. Although there are always six quarter notes per measure, they may, however, be distributed in two ways. In some airs there is almost always an eighth note between two quarter notes and in others, there are several quarter notes and several eighth notes in a row, indiscriminately mixed with half notes.

First Way

Second Way

These two ways of distributing the notes in 6/4 time establish a difference in the manner of beating time which we will explain later.[7]

Six-Eight Time Signature

After having learned what the time signatures require in regard to the number of notes in each measure of a piece, one must learn what they require regarding the manner of beating time and of giving the tempo. This has to do with a matter that I touched on previously in the place where I spoke of the way to regulate the duration of notes [ch. IV, p. 24] in saying that quarter notes should be measured by the steps of a man who walks one and a quarter leagues in an hour, and that the other note values are determined in proportion to the quarter note. But what I said there is not a rule which must be applied to all kinds of pieces, for if that were the case, they would have too great a uniformity of tempo between them, since the notes in all of them would move at the same speed. However, there are several types of movement, and thus it is necessary that quarter notes and the other notes in proportion move with a certain speed in

---

7. See p. 38 in this chapter. St Lambert's first way of distributing notes in 6/4 time is a common rhythmic pattern in a gigue, loure, or canarie. The second is found in various types of composition, e.g. the second part of a French opera overture.

certain pieces and with another speed in other pieces. If I did not make this distinction in the preceding pages, it is because there wasn't enough time to discuss it then, and if besides I chose the steps of a man who walks one and a quarter leagues in an hour for the duration of quarter notes, it is because this tempo is more usual for quarter notes, and there are fewer pieces in which they move at another speed. I will explain these different levels of speed indicated by the time signatures in order while teaching how to beat time, for these two things are connected to each other. But it must be observed that what I am about to say regarding the manner of beating time cannot be done while playing the harpsichord or any other instrument, since the hands are occupied, and only those who sing can do it. However, I don't believe I should absolve myself from speaking of it, since it is a useful thing to know for anyone who gets involved in music, and besides there is no other means of teaching how rhythm is given to pieces, which it is absolutely necessary to know.

For the Major Time Signature C

In pieces marked with the major time signature, the measure is beaten in four, that is to say one must make four hand movements for each measure. They are usually made with the right hand for the sake of grace. The first beat is made by lowering the hand or by striking it in the left hand, the second by carrying it to the right, the third by passing it to the left, and the fourth by raising it, imitating with these four motions the figure seen here.

These four movements must be equal, that is, one must not take more time going from the first to the second than from the second to the third, from the third to the fourth, and from the fourth to the first. The four-beat measure is very slow [*fort grave*]; the beats should be measured by the steps of a man taking a walk, and fairly slowly at that. I always compare the beats in music to the steps of a man, because being equal between themselves they are very appropriate for giving a correct idea of the beats and their equality. There are four quarter notes in quadruple time, thus each quarter note must last one beat. The half notes must last two beats, the dotted halves three, and the whole notes four. The eighth notes must only last half a beat, that is, two must go by in the time of one beat, and since the sixteenth notes have half again the value of the eighths, there are four of them per beat. But all this has already been said in the chapter concerning note values.

The first note of the measure is played while beating the first beat. If it is a quarter note, it lasts from the first beat to the second, if a half note from the first to the third, etc. But sometimes the first note is not played with the first beat, as will be seen later in Chapter X [Concerning Rests].

For the Minor Time Signature ₵

In pieces marked with the minor time signature, the measure is beaten in two, the first beat made by lowering the hand, which is called *frapper* [to beat] and the second by raising it, according to this figure.

This measure contains four quarter notes, as does the major time signature, and thus in order to make an equal division of the two beats it is necessary to give two quarter notes to each one.

The two hand motions made in beating this measure must be equal in duration to those made in the four-beat measure, that is, neither slower nor faster, and this means that in pieces in the minor time signature the notes go twice as fast as in pieces marked with the major time signature, since two quarter notes instead of one are put in the time of one beat.

In pieces in this tempo, the speed of the quarter notes goes back to the one I gave them earlier when I based them on the steps of a man who goes one and a quarter leagues in an hour.

For the Binary Time Signature 2

In pieces in binary time, the measure is beaten in two, as in those pieces marked ¢, but with the difference that the beats in binary time must go twice as fast as those in ¢. With that exception the two types of meter are completely alike.⁸

For the Time Signature $\frac{4}{8}$

In pieces in $\frac{4}{8}$ time, the measure is also beaten in two, but as each measure only contains four eighth notes and as there are only two eighths to put on each beat and not two quarter notes as there were in the preceding meters, these beats must go twice again as fast as those in binary time. Thus this meter is very fast [*très vîte*].

8. Not all of St Lambert's contemporaries agreed with him on this point; see Translator's Introduction, pp. xvii-xviii.

For the Time Signature $\frac{3}{2}$

In pieces in $\frac{3}{2}$ time, the measure is beaten in three. The first beat is made by striking, that is by lowering the hand, the second by carrying it to the right, and the third by raising it, as shown in this figure.⁹

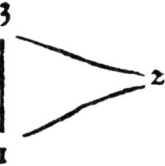

A measure in $\frac{3}{2}$ contains three half notes, one of which or its equivalent is placed on each beat. The beats must be grave, that is slow, and exactly equal to those in the four-beat measure.

For the Ternary Time Signature 3

In pieces in ternary time, the measure is beaten in three as for the preceding meter, except that in this one the beats must go twice as fast because the measure is only made up of three quarter notes, one of which or its equivalent is placed on each beat. With that exception these two

9. This triangular figure for beating triple time, and the crossing figure given above for quadruple time, represent important changes in the mechanics of beating time. Most earlier theorists had beaten all the different meters by a simple lowering and raising of the hand. For example, the four-beat measure was usually beaten with two downstrokes followed by two upstrokes, the three-beat measure either by two downstrokes followed by an upstroke, or by a single downstroke held for two beats followed by an upstroke (*tactus inaequalis*). For a discussion of 17th-century theory regarding beating time, see George Houle, 'The musical measure as discussed by theorists from 1650 to 1800', (Ph.D. dissertation, Stanford University, 1960).

meters are completely alike, but this one is much more in use than the other, as we will observe later.

In pieces in this tempo the quarter notes once again have the duration of the steps of a man who walks one and a quarter leagues in one hour.

For the Time Signature $\frac{3}{8}$

In pieces in $\frac{3}{8}$ time, the measure is also beaten in three, but since this meter is made up of only three eighth notes, there being only one eighth note to put on each beat, the beats must go twice again as fast as those of the ternary time signature, that is to say very fast [*très vîte*]. But because of this very fast tempo and the difficulty there would be in making three hand movements so quickly, it is customary to beat this meter in one. One simply lowers the hand on the first beat of each measure and passes over the others by raising it without distinguishing the second or third beats.

It is in this way that all menuets for dancing are beaten, even though the measure is made up of three quarter notes, since they are played very quickly [*fort gayement*]. I say menuets for dancing because there are harpsichord menuets which are not ordinarily played as fast as this.[10]

For the Time Signature $\frac{6}{4}$

In pieces in $\frac{6}{4}$ time, the measure is beaten in two ways, as we said above. When the notes are distributed in the measure in the manner I called the first way, an example of which can be seen above [p. 35], the measure is beaten in two, on each of which beats three quarter notes or their equivalent are placed. But when these notes are distributed in the manner I call the second way, the measure is beaten in three, not in three slow beats by placing two quarter notes on each beat as in $\frac{3}{2}$ time, but in three quick beats like those in triple time [3],[11] by placing only one quarter note on each beat and thus making two measures out of one, since there are six quarter notes per measure.

The quarter notes in this meter, when it is beaten in three, go back again to the steps of the man I have spoken of so much.[12] But when it is beaten in two, the notes go by much faster, for these two beats must be at least as fast as those in binary time [2].[13]

For the Time Signature $\frac{6}{8}$

In pieces in $\frac{6}{8}$ time, the measure is also beaten in two, just as is the first way of beating $\frac{6}{4}$, except that the beats must go twice as fast as those in $\frac{6}{4}$ because the measure is only composed of six eighth notes instead of six quarters. With that exception, there is no difference between these two meters.

The movements made with the hand while beating time must not be done limply. On the contrary, they must be perceptibly and distinctly marked, and even though they are done in the air it must appear as if one were beating on something, as the word *beat* itself implies. The hand must, so to speak, dance while doing them and represent for the eyes an image of

---

10. The slower tempo is due to the greater amount of ornamentation and figuration in harpsichord menuets by composers such as d'Anglebert.

11. The original erroneously says 'binary time' (2).
12. In other words, the quarter note in the second type of $\frac{6}{4}$, that is in pieces such as the second section of some French overtures, is exactly equal to the quarter note in 3.
13. I.e. ♩ in this type of $\frac{6}{4}$ is equal to or faster than ♩ in 2.

the rhythm that the ear must hear. But the first beat of every measure must be still more marked than the others. Musicians call this beat the *frappé* because as a matter of fact those who beat time in an ensemble are accustomed to beating this downbeat on their hands or on a table with a piece of rolled paper.[14] Thus one makes the first beat of the measure more perceptible than the others because it is always on this beat that the *cadence* falls in an air, and it is in order to mark its fall that one beats the *frappé* with vigor. But as it is impossible to beat time with the hand while playing the harpsichord, the player must fill his head with the idea of these movements in order to beat time mentally and to regulate, according to the time beating in his head, the rhythm of the pieces he plays.

Not all the types of meter we have just discussed are in equal use. The most common are:

The meter
{
of two grave or slow [*graves ou lents*] beats, marked by the minor time signature [¢];
of two lively or quick [*gais ou légers*] beats, marked by the binary time signature [2];
of three quick [*légers*] beats, marked by the triple time signature [3].
}

This is why when musicians speak of an air in duple time they always mean an air marked with the minor or binary time signatures [¢ or 2], and never an air in $\frac{4}{8}$ time, or still less in $\frac{6}{4}$ or $\frac{6}{8}$, even though these last two are also beaten in two.

In the same way, when they speak of an air simply in triple time, they mean an air marked with the ternary time signature [3], but when they say three slow beats, that means $\frac{3}{2}$ time.

In regard to airs marked with other time signatures, musicians normally call them by the name of the time signature. For example, they speak of an air in $\frac{6}{4}$ or $\frac{3}{8}$, etc., unless these airs have particular names which distinguish them better than the time signature. Then they use these names and speak of a gigue, a passepied, etc.[15]

I made this comment here so that the reader will understand what I mean when I speak of an air in duple time or an air in triple time, as I am going to do in the following section.

Concerning Some Difficulties that are Found in the Manner of Beating Time

It is easy to beat time in a piece when the number of notes in each measure is equal to the number of beats that must be made in order to beat time, as when for example, in a piece in triple time, there are always three quarter notes per measure. But when the number of notes does not correspond to the number of beats and there are either more notes than beats, or more

---

14. This type of audible time-keeping was commonly practiced in France as a means of keeping the musicians in a large ensemble together. A 1709 English translation of Raguenet's *Parallèle des Italiens et des François en ce qui regarde la Musique et les Opéras* speaks of the typical Parisian director who beat time 'on a Table put there for that purpose, so loud, that he made a greater Noise than the Whole Band' (cited in Adam Carse, *The Orchestra in the 18th Century* (Cambridge, 1940), p. 103). At the Opéra in Paris the time-beater generally used a large stick which he beat on the floor, and tradition has it that Jean-Baptiste Lully died from the gangrene that set in after he struck his foot with his stick. The roll of paper mentioned by St Lambert came to be a symbol of the director's authority and a number of 17th- and 18th-century composers and choirmasters, including Lully, may be seen in portraits holding one in their hands. This type of time-beating did not include the interpretive functions of today's orchestral conductor.

15. The time signatures associated with the most common dance types of the late 17th century are as follows: allemande ¢ ; sarabande, passacaille, chaconne, and menuet, 3; courante $\frac{3}{2}$ (but also 3 even when $\frac{3}{2}$ is understood. See below, p. 45); gaillarde $\frac{3}{2}$; loure $\frac{6}{4}$; bourée, rigaudon, and gavotte, ¢ or 2; gigue $\frac{6}{4}$, $\frac{6}{8}$, $\frac{12}{8}$, or 3; canaries $\frac{6}{4}$, $\frac{6}{8}$, or 3; passepied $\frac{3}{8}$ or $\frac{6}{8}$.

beats than notes, it is a little more difficult to adjust them to each other. However, this is not the greatest difficulty that can occur in the manner of beating time. The most awkward thing for people learning how to beat time is when there happen to be compound notes in a measure which anticipate from one beat to another, that is notes which, having entirely filled the beat on which they began, complete their value on the first half or quarter of the following beat. It is necessary to give some examples of these notes, in order to explain how they are adjusted to the beats.

(Those who do not know how to sing should play the following notes on the keyboard with the left hand, and beat time with the right.[16])

Note A is played while beating the first beat of the measure, but since it is worth a beat and a half because it is dotted, the second beat is also beaten before leaving this note. After having beaten the second beat, note B is played before beating the third beat, because note B takes up the rest of the second beat of which note A only occupied the first half. Then the third beat is beaten on note C.

Another Example

16. It is indicative of Saint Lambert's pedagogical thoroughness that the musical examples in this chapter, which up to this point had been notated mainly for the treble, are written from here on for the left hand, in order to free the right hand for beating time.

On the compound note D, the first, second, and third beats are beaten. After the third beat is beaten, note E is played before falling onto the first beat of the following measure.

The Same Thing Notated in Another Way

Another Example

The first and second beats are beaten on the compound note F, but as soon as the second beat is beaten, one plays the three notes G, H, and I before beating the third beat on note K.

Another Example

The compound note L is worth two measures plus a beat and a half; thus on this note the entire first and second measures are beaten along with the first and second beat of the third, but after beating the second beat of the third measure, note M is played before beating the third beat, which is only beaten while playing note N.

Concerning Syncopation

There is another kind of anticipation, still more awkward than the one we just discussed. This is when a note starts at the middle of one beat and ends at the middle of another. These types of notes are called syncopations, and the measures where they are found syncopated measures. But without concerning oneself with the name, it is only necessary to note that syncopation is found almost exclusively in duple time [₵ or 2], although it may also be occasionally used in other meters. In order to make this syncopated measure easy to beat, one must form another idea of it than the one offered at first to the eyes. To explain this I will give some examples.

EXAMPLE OF SYNCOPATION

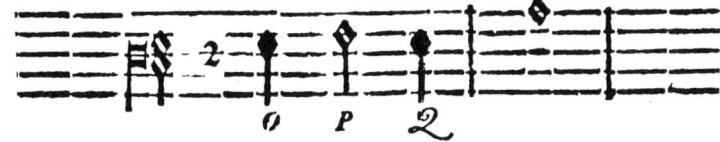

Explanation

The half note P is the one which syncopates. It begins its value halfway through the first beat of the measure it is in and finishes it halfway through the second. In order to beat this measure, one must lower the hand for the first beat of note O, then play note P and after having played it when half of its value is consumed, one must raise the hand for the second beat. The other half of note P makes the beginning of the second beat and this beat is concluded by playing note Q. This is how this measure is beaten, but it will be easier to do by considering note P as if it were two quarter notes tied together instead of one half note, because one sees two quarter notes to put on each beat.

Syncopation is found more often in quick duple time [2] than in slow duple time [₵]. It also sometimes appears in quadruple time [C] and in $\frac{4}{8}$, but it is found only very rarely in the other meters. Wherever it is found it is performed, as I said, by beating the beat at the midpoint of its value. But in order to do it with greater facility, it is necessary to divide the syncopated note in half in one's mind. If it is a whole note, consider it as two tied half notes; if it is a quarter note, as two tied eighths.

EXAMPLE OF SYNCOPATIONS IN QUADRUPLE AND FOUR-EIGHT TIME

(The starred notes are the syncopated ones)

The manner in which it is necessary to imagine these notes in order to adjust them to the beats without difficulty [is as follows]:

Anticipation from one beat to the next by means of syncopation is almost exclusively found, as I said before, in duple time. But the kind of anticipation by means of dotted notes or those connected by a tie is found in all meters. However, I only gave examples of these in triple time [p. 40], but whoever understands how these anticipated notes are beaten in triple time will easily understand how they are beaten in other meters, for in all types of meter the notes are adjusted to the beats in the same way.

In order to understand in a single idea everything we have said concerning the meters, we will observe that they may be reduced to three types. The first includes those that are composed of four notes, that is:

Meters $\begin{cases} \text{Major, marked by } \mathbf{C} \\ \text{Minor, marked by } \mathbf{\phi} \\ \text{Binary, marked by 2} \\ \text{Four-Eight, marked by } \frac{4}{8} \end{cases}$

The second type includes those that are composed of three notes, that is:

Meters $\begin{cases} \text{Three-Two, marked by } \frac{3}{2} \\ \text{Triple, marked by 3} \\ \text{Three-Eight, marked by } \frac{3}{8} \end{cases}$

The third type includes those that are composed of six notes, that is:

Meters $\begin{cases} \text{Six-Four, marked by } \frac{6}{4} \\ \text{Six-Eight, marked by } \frac{6}{8}* \end{cases}$

After having distinguished three types of meter, it is possible to consider the gradations of tempo which follow the order in which the meters are arranged above.

* *Remark on Meter*: Besides the different types of meter we discussed in Chapter VIII, there are some masters who admit several others, such as:

Meters $\begin{cases} \text{Twelve-Four, composed of twelve quarter notes} \\ \text{and indicated by the numbers } \frac{12}{4}; \\ \text{Twelve-Eight, composed of twelve eighth notes} \\ \text{and indicated by } \frac{12}{8}; \\ \text{Nine-Four, composed of nine quarter notes and} \\ \text{indicated by } \frac{9}{4}; \\ \text{Nine-Eight, composed of nine eighth notes and} \\ \text{indicated by } \frac{9}{8}. \end{cases}$

But these meters are so rare in our music[17] that I have not yet seen any airs composed in any of them except for three in $\frac{12}{8}$ time: two ☞

17. I.e. French music.

The major time signature gives pieces a grave and slow tempo [*un mouvement grave et lent*], as explained in the preceding pages, and when it is well understood, it explains all the meters of the first type, for the minor time signature gives pieces a tempo twice as fast as the major sign does, the binary twice as fast as the minor, and $\frac{4}{8}$ twice as fast as the binary.

In the second group, the time signature $\frac{3}{2}$ indicates a very slow tempo [*un mouvement fort grave*] for pieces, parallel in its kind to that of the major time signature, as was explained before. The ternary time signature gives them a tempo twice as fast, and $\frac{3}{8}$ a tempo twice as fast as the ternary.

☞ gigues by M. d'Anglebert[18] and the beautiful Italian air from *l'Europe galante*, 'Ad un cuore'.[19]

The extreme rarity of these meters is what prevented me from placing them among the ranks of those I discussed in the method book, but since it is necessary as much as possible to leave nothing to be desired by those one wishes to instruct, I will teach how to beat these meters here, even though they are not in common use.

There is no meter, no matter what kind it is, that cannot be beaten in two, three or four; since the number of notes the measure contains can only be even or odd, the total value of the measure can always be divided into two, three, or four equal units. On this principle, measures in $\frac{12}{4}$ or $\frac{12}{8}$ time are beaten in two or in four, as one pleases, but better four than two, placing three quarter notes or their equivalent on each beat in $\frac{12}{4}$ and three eighth notes in $\frac{12}{8}$. Measures in $\frac{9}{4}$ or $\frac{9}{8}$ are necessarily beaten in three, placing three quarter notes on each beat in the former and three eighths in the latter.

18. Jean Henry d'Anglebert, *Pièces de clavecin*. Facsimile of the 1689 Paris edition (New York: Broude Bros., 1965), pp. 15-16 and 47-8.
19. *L'Europe galante*, opera-ballet by André Campra, first performed in 1697. 'Ad un cuore' may be found on pp. 174-5 of the score published by Ballard in 1724.

In the third group, the time signature $\frac{6}{4}$ requires a very lively tempo [*un mouvement fort gay*] for pieces, especially when the measure is beaten in two. But $\frac{6}{8}$ gives them a tempo twice as fast, that is to say very fast [*très vîte*].[20]

These are the rules established in music concerning the tempo of pieces, but of all the rules of this art, these are the least observed by those who profess it. That which is commonly said of painters and poets, that they take licences, may also be said of musicians. The later transgress the rules of music just as the others do those of painting and poetry. But it is particularly in regard to the tempo of pieces that musicians take liberties against their principles. Every trained musician who plays a piece composed by someone else does not attempt so much to give this piece the tempo that the composer tried to indicate by the time signature he placed

20. The proportionality of tempo implied by the time signatures in St Lambert's system can be seen in the chart below. The metronome value of 120 for the steps of St Lambert's walking man is by no means an absolute figure but represents an approximate value based on the length of the French league in 1702 and the probable length of stride of the man in question. It is also supported by evidence from other 18th-century sources. For a discussion of St Lambert's tempo system, including the derivation of this value, see the Translator's Introduction, pp. xvff.

♩ in **C** = 60	𝅗𝅥 in $\frac{3}{2}$ = 60	
♩ in ¢ = 120	♩ in **3** = 120	♩ in $\frac{6}{4}$ (2nd way) = 120
𝅗𝅥 in **2** = 120		𝅗𝅥. in $\frac{6}{4}$ (1st way) = 120
♩ in $\frac{4}{8}$ = 240	♪ in $\frac{3}{8}$ = 240	♩. in $\frac{6}{8}$ = 240

at the beginning, as to give it one which satisfies his own taste. He is brought to this point because he is convinced that no matter how much trouble he gives himself, he will only be able to discover the true intention of the composer by chance. He clearly sees that the composer of the piece has indicated by the time signature whether one should play it slowly [*gravement*] or quickly [*gayement*], but he doesn't know precisely what the composer means by *gravement* or *gayement*, because one person may mean one thing, another something else. In order to know rightly the true meaning of the time signatures in regard to tempo, it would be necessary for all musicians to gather together and in a general concert by means of a demonstration addressed to the eyes, or rather the ears of all, to come to an agreement as to what is meant by the tempo of the major time signature, the minor time signature, and the others. After that there would be no more ambiguity, at least not for those who had been present at the assembly, and for them the time signatures would be sure indications of the tempo of pieces. But this so useful concert being impossible to do, their meaning will always remain confused. For myself I have fixed it as much as possible in the method book by the comparison I gave of a man walking sometimes slowly, sometimes fast. But what I was able to communicate by this comparison is not definite enough yet. For when I said that in certain pieces that I specified, the quarter notes by which the tempo of pieces is regulated must have the duration of the steps of a man who walks one and a quarter leagues in an hour, the matter is not clearly decided just because of that. Since men are not all the same size, a tall man walks less quickly in order to go one and a quarter leagues in an hour than another man who is shorter; thus the steps of the former will be slower than those of the latter. And although what I said is based on a medium-sized man, the measure that I tried to give in this way is still only confusedly explained.[21] Thus I don't so much claim by this comparison to have given the true measure of the duration of the quarter notes as I hope to have given the idea of the equality they must have, which is the most important aspect of movement. But even if I had positively explained the tempo of each time signature, which cannot be done in a book, my decision would perhaps not be approved by all teachers. One might find, for example, that I had given the major time signature too slow a tempo, and another on the contrary would find it too lively, for everyone follows his own taste in these matters, as in many other things. Musicians, however, all use the same terms. They all call the tempo of the major time signature a slow, grave tempo; that of binary and ternary time a lively tempo; and all the rest by the same names that I gave them in this chapter. But even though they all use the same terminology, they do not all understand it in the same way. This is experienced every day by those who play airs from operas on the harpsichord without having heard how they are performed at the Opéra;[22] for they give these airs the tempo they think is appropriate to them and which they have judged from the time signatures marking them. Going later to the Opéra, they hear these airs played at another

---

21. St Lambert was apparently unaware of the efforts of another French theorist, Étienne Loulié, in developing an accurate device for indicating tempo. Loulié's chronometer, a pendulum of variable length described in his *Elements of Music* of 1696, was the first practicable metronome-like device. During the course of the 18th century, a number of theorists and musicians in France made use of this machine, or improved versions of it, to indicate the tempo of a sizeable number of pieces. See Eugène Borrel, 'Les indications métronomiques laissées par les auteurs français du 18e siècle', *Revue de Musicologie* (1928), 149-53, and the same author's *Interprétation de la musique française (de Lully à la Révolution)*, (Paris, 1934); Ralph Kirkpatrick, '18th-century metronomic indications', *Papers of the AMS*, (1938), 30-50; Neal Zaslaw, 'Materials for the life and works of Jean-Marie Leclair l'aîné' (Ph.D. dissertation, Columbia University, 1970), 240-63; Rebecca Harris-Warrick, 'The tempo of French baroque dances: evidence from 18th-century metronome devices', *Proceedings of the 1982 Meeting of the Dance History Scholars*, (Cambridge, Mass., 1982), 18-27.

22. St Lambert means the Opéra in Paris, officially known as the Académie Royale de Musique, which was housed in the Palais Royal.

tempo than the ones they gave them. The time signatures thus indicate the tempo of pieces only very imperfectly, and musicians who recognize this drawback often add one of the following words to the time signature in the pieces they compose: *Lentement, Gravement, Légèrement, Gayement, Vîte, Fort Vîte*, and the like, in order to compensate for the inability of the time signature to express their intention.[23]

The imprecise meaning of the time signatures is a defect in the art for which musicians are not responsible and which may easily be pardoned them. But the one thing for which they could be rightly reproached is that often the same man marks two airs of completely differing tempo with the same time signature, as for example M. de Lully, who has the reprise of the overture to *Armide* played very fast and the air on page 93 of the same opera played very slowly, even though this air and the reprise of the overture are both marked with the time signature $\frac{6}{4}$, and both have six quarter notes per measure distributed in the same way.[24] I don't mean to condemn M. de Lully on this account; he was able to take this liberty because his art permitted him to do so; but I wish that musicians themselves would correct this imperfection in music which results in theory being belied by practice.

But the liberty which musicians give themselves of transgressing their own rules goes even farther than I have just pointed out; it goes as far as not marking pieces with their true time signature. All our harpsichord masters only put the simple triple time signature 3 in courantes, when they ought to use $\frac{3}{2}$, since the measure is composed of three half notes and not three quarter notes.[25] It is true that there are some courantes in which the measure can be beaten in a quick three by making two measures out of one, and it seems that this is what these musicians intend when they mark them only with the simple triple,[26] but however they intend it, this still goes against the rule, for if they want these pieces to be beaten in a quick three, they should cut the measures in half; and if they intend them to be beaten in a slow three, they must mark them in $\frac{3}{2}$.

From all this I conclude that since people are so inexact in music in observing the rules of time signatures and tempo, the reader who studies the principles of the harpsichord here should not dwell very much on everything I have said on the subject. He may avail himself of the musician's privilege and give pieces whatever tempo pleases him without paying more than passing attention to the time signature which marks it, provided that he not choose a tempo opposite to the one demanded by the time signature, which could remove all grace from the piece, but rather that he choose one which is appropriate and shows the piece to advantage. He should especially observe what musicians call meter, that is, the rhythm of the piece, which consists of playing notes of the same value with complete equality of movement, and all the notes with equality of proportion, for whether a piece is played slowly or fast, one must always give it the rhythm which is its soul and the thing it can least do without.

23. See p. 93, where St Lambert felt the necessity to clarify his own intention by adding the word *lentement* to a musical example with the time signature 3.

24. St Lambert's page reference is to the score of Lully's opera *Armide* that was published by Christophe Ballard in 1686. The two pieces may be seen in appendix A, pp. 110-11. The reprise of the overture has no tempo marking, but the air is marked *gravement*. Although at first glance the two pieces appear to fall into the two different categories of $\frac{6}{4}$, St Lambert was probably thinking of them as belonging to what he calls the second way of distributing the notes (see p. 35).

25. This remark is accurate. Chambonnières and d'Anglebert consistently give courantes a time signature of 3 even though there are six quarter notes per measure. Nor are courantes the only dances to reveal such traces of the old mensural notation. Gigues, for example, are sometimes found written in 3 when the signature should be $\frac{6}{4}$, pavannes in C instead of $\frac{4}{2}$.

26. At best some courantes can be beaten in a quick 3 for a few measures in a row, but the continuous interplay between duple and triple divisions of the measure in the courante belies this statement of St Lambert's. For once, however, a notational reform supported by St Lambert did take effect: $\frac{3}{2}$ became standardized as the time signature for the French courante.

The equality of movement that we require in notes of the same value is not observed with eighth notes when there are several in a row. The practice is to make them alternately long and short, because this inequality gives them more grace. If the number of eighth notes which follow each other without interruption is even, the first note is long, the second short, the third long, the fourth short, and so on with the others until the end, even if there are a hundred in a row. If the number of notes is odd, the first, on the contrary, is short, the second long, the third short, the fourth long, the fifth short, etc., until the end.[27] A single eighth note is always short, but when there are two in a row the first is long and the second short because the number is even.

However, this inequality of several consecutive eighth notes is not observed in pieces in quadruple time [C], as for example in allemandes, because of the slow tempo. Then the inequality falls on the sixteenth notes, if there are any.

In pieces that are in slow triple meter [$^3_2$], if there happen to be several quarter notes in a row, they are made unequal like eighth notes. See the vocal duet in *Phaéton* whose words are: 'Hélas! une chaîne si belle'.[28] Other than these instances, all the notes of the same value are played equally.

When one must make the eighth or quarter notes unequal, it is a matter of taste to decide if they should be more or less unequal. There are some pieces in which it is appropriate to make them very unequal and others in which they should be less so. Taste is the judge of this, as of tempo.[29]

Before finishing this chapter, it would be a good idea to point out that what we said several pages ago, that each measure of a piece contains an equal number of notes relative to their value, must be understood assuming that the piece doesn't change meter, for there are some pieces that don't keep the same one from beginning to end. They sometimes start in duple time and in the middle they change to triple, or another meter, or having had triple time at the beginning they end in duple. Sometimes the same piece changes meter three or four times. There are very few opera overtures that do not change three times, and in recitative the meter varies constantly.[30] This change of meter is rarer in harpsichord pieces than in opera airs, but wherever it is found it is indicated by a new time signature put in the place where the piece must change.

Example

Operas are full of this type of example, so I won't give any more here; but I will point out that there are certain pieces whose first and last measures are incomplete and are only worth one measure between the two of them. These pieces are more usually written in duple time than other-

---

27. If the number of notes is odd, the first falls on an upbeat and is therefore short.

28. *Phaéton, tragédie lyrique* by J.-B. Lully, first performed in 1683. The duet 'Une chaîne si belle' is found in Act V, Sc. 3. It contains several melismas of stepwise quarter notes on the word *chaîne*.

29. See the Remark in ch. IV, p. 25, for additional comments on inequality.

30. The problem of determining the relationships of note values between meters in French recitative is indeed thorny. St Lambert's statements on the proportionality of meter provide an important piece of evidence, although certain ideas of his have doubtful applicability to recitative. See R. Peter Wolf, 'Metrical relationships in French recitative of the 17th and 18th centuries', *Recherches* 18 (1978), 29-49, and Robert Fajon, 'Propositions pour une analyse rationalisée du récitatif de l'opéra lullyste', *Revue de Musicologie*, 64 (1978), 55-75.

wise. The first measure has only two quarter notes or their equivalent, and the last has the two others; or, the first having only one, the last has three. But no matter what the time signature of the piece, if something is missing from the first measure to make it complete, the remainder is always in the last, and both joined together make only one measure.

EXAMPLE OF PIECES WHOSE FIRST MEASURE IS NOT COMPLETE

In Slow Duple Time

In Quick Duple Time

In Triple Time

In Six-Four Time

In Six-Eight Time

When pieces like these begin with half a measure, as in the examples of slow duple and $\frac{6}{8}$ time above, and if the measure is beaten in two as in these same examples, one must start to beat with the upbeat and not with the downbeat, as one does in other pieces. But if the piece starts with a quarter or a third of a measure, or sometimes less, as in the other examples, then one only starts to beat on the first note of the first complete measure. That which precedes it is played or sung while holding the hand in the air ready to fall on the first beat of the measure. Allemandes, courantes, gigues, rigaudons, and bourées are pieces of this last type.

CHAPTER IX

Concerning the Voices

(Des Parties)

In earlier times, music was not the same as we practice it today. There was only a single melody, accommodated to the meaning and the rhythm of the poetry that was sung, and the instruments that were played created but a single voice. Now the practice is to bring several voices, that is several sounds, together, and this mixture of several sounds in accord with each other is called harmony. This recent type of music is much more perfect than the earlier kind, for it includes the earlier one in its entirety with everything beautiful it has to offer and also adds the harmony of the voices, without which in my opinion music is not music. There are some instruments which maintain the earlier practice and on which only one part can be played, such as flutes, oboes, violins, etc. But the harpsichord has the advantage that one may play several voices at the same time and that a man all alone is capable of being his own little ensemble.

The number of voices in music is not limited. One may compose pieces of six, seven, eight, and even more voices. However, these are ordinarily reduced to four, to which the following names are given: the lowest is called the *basse* [bass], the highest the *dessus* [treble], the closest to the *dessus* the *haute-contre* [alto], and the closest to the *basse* the *taille* [tenor]. Here they are in order:

Dessus
Haute-Contre
Taille
Basse

When one composes in five parts, the fifth part is called the *quinte* [quintus] and is placed between the tenor and the bass in this order:

Dessus
Haute-Contre
Taille
Quinte
Basse[1]

If one composes in six, seven, or eight parts, then only the treble and bass are distinguished by name. The other voices which could have an individual name are only included under the general name of inner voices, or simply voices.

1. This five-part distribution represents the typical French orchestral texture of the 17th and early 18th centuries. The *dessus* was played by violins, the *basse* by *basses de violons*, and the inner parts by violas of different sizes. See J. Eppelsheim, *Das Orchester in den Werken Jean-Baptiste Lullys* (Tutzing, 1961); also the two orchestral excerpts from Lully's *Armide* in appendix A (pp. 110-11).

Note to the Reader

Since the word staff [*portée*] used in the following passage is not familiar to everyone, I thought it necessary to explain its meaning before using it. By staff is meant the five parallel lines which frame the pitches of the notes and which we called the *échelle* of music at the beginning of this book [ch. I, p. 9]. When these five lines are repeated six times on one page, the paper which contains them is called six-staff paper. If they are repeated eight or twelve times, it is called eight- or twelve-staff paper, and so on.

In harpsichord scores, the staves are divided two by two on each page. On the upper staff are placed the treble and the voices nearest it, and on the lower staff the bass and its nearest voices, set one above the other in a vertical line, as seen in the example below.

The voices arranged in the upper staff are played by the right hand and are called without distinction the treble voices in general. Those on the lower staff are played with the left hand and are also called in general and without distinction the basses. However, the true treble of a piece is always the highest voice played by the right hand, and the true bass is the lowest voice played by the left hand.

Nothing is more irregular than harpsichord pieces in regard to the number of voices. The same piece sometimes has four voices, sometimes six, sometimes two, sometimes three, sometimes eight, etc. This irregularity is in the spirit of the instrument, and in it lies one of the greatest beauties of harpsichord pieces.[2]

---

2. This discontinuity of texture is indeed one of the most salient characteristics of late 17th-century French harpsichord music. For an excellent discussion of this style, see David Fuller, 'Eighteenth-century French harpsichord music' (Ph.D. dissertation, Harvard University, 1965), pp. 36-63.

A LITTLE PIECE TO SERVE AS AN EXAMPLE OF EVERYTHING JUST SAID CONCERNING THE VOICES

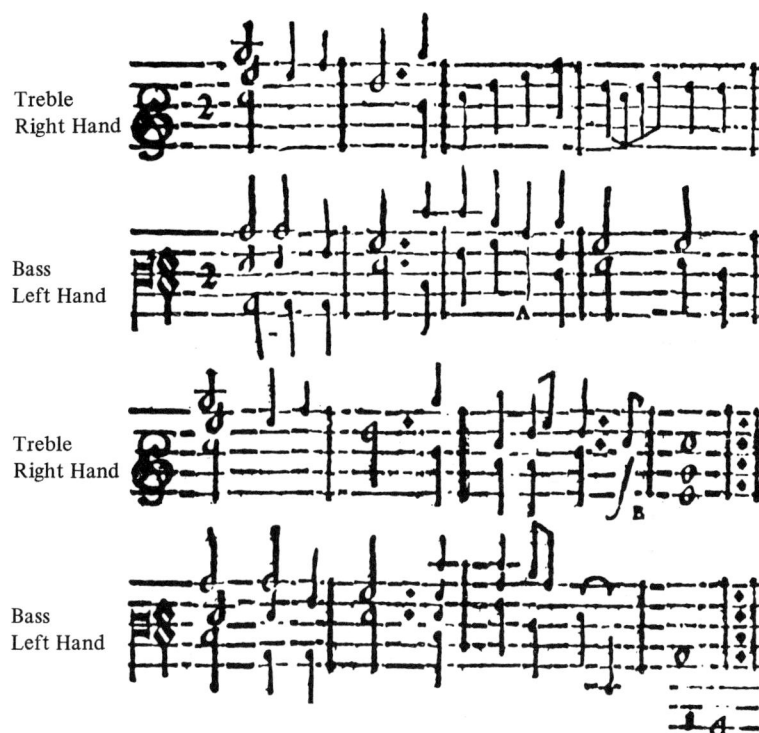

Since we said in the preceding chapter that the binary time signature [2] only required four quarter notes or their equivalent per measure, the reader will perhaps be surprised to find more in the measures of the little piece given above. But it is necessary to know that when one says that there are four quarter notes per measure, that means four quarter notes in

each voice. Since in harpsichord pieces there is more than one voice in a measure, there must be more than four quarter notes per measure. However, there are not always as many times four beats per measure as there are voices one above the other in some places, because, as I said, not all the voices in a piece continue regularly from beginning to end, and the inner voices are added or removed at the will of the composer, as the arrangement of the treble and bass permit. Thus the treble and bass always have the number of notes required by the time signature, but the other voices enter and leave the measure in greater or lesser numbers without any considerations of regularity in order to form chords in only some places, as required by the spirit of the harpsichord.

If you examine the preceding little piece, you will see that it starts with a six-voice chord, but that as of the second beat of the first measure, two of the voices played by the right hand drop out, and that in the second measure the basses lose one of their voices, the texture being reduced to three voices at that place. A fourth voice enters, however, with the following chord, and then the texture is reduced to only two voices on the second beat of the third measure. Thus it is that harpsichord pieces are irregular in the number of voices, which is more appropriate to them than an exact continuation of each one.

Notes that have two stems, as in the preceding example at A and B, signify that two voices come together on the same pitch in that place.

Sometimes these double-stemmed notes also have double heads and are simultaneously a half note and a quarter note (see C, in the example below), or a whole note and a quarter (D), or an eighth note and a quarter (E), etc. In this case their length is determined by the larger note value, thus holding a whole note and a quarter as long as a single whole note, a half note and a quarter as long as a single half note, and a quarter and an eighth as long as a single quarter note, etc.:

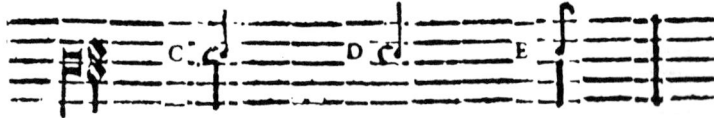

But even though a double note is held for as long as the larger note value requires, one nevertheless does not wait for this longer note value to be over before playing the following note. On the contrary, the following note is played as soon as the smaller note value of the double note has expired.

CHAPTER X

Concerning Rests

(Des Pauses)

Rests are symbols or characters used to notate the silences which must sometimes be observed in certain voices of pieces, and sometimes in all voices. But as everything in music is regulated by the beat, the silences have a specific duration determined by their symbols, after which one resumes playing or singing. As there are five kinds of notes, so are there five kinds of rests, because the duration of the rests is measured by the duration of the notes.

NAMES AND DEMONSTRATION OF THE RESTS

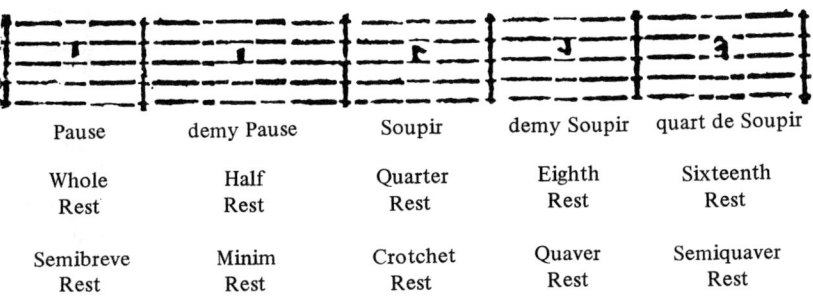

Pause	demy Pause	Soupir	demy Soupir	quart de Soupir
Whole Rest	Half Rest	Quarter Rest	Eighth Rest	Sixteenth Rest
Semibreve Rest	Minim Rest	Crotchet Rest	Quaver Rest	Semiquaver Rest

Since whole and half rests are so similar in shape, one might possibly not notice the difference between them without being advised of it. It is only that the whole rest is attached [to the line] from above and the half rest from below, or in other words, that the whole rest is always under a line and the half rest above.[1] The quarter, eighth, and sixteenth rests are not attached to anything and the difference between them is evident from their shapes.

The whole rest is worth a whole note, that is, it indicates a silence which must last as long as the time taken to express a whole note. The half rest is worth a half note, the quarter rest a quarter note, the eighth rest an eighth note, and the sixteenth rest a sixteenth note.

Since several voices are played simultaneously on the harpsichord, people who are not trained in music never notice that there are rests in pieces, because it is rare for there to be a rest in all the voices at once, and when one voice is silent, there is always another which is speaking. But even though rests are almost imperceptible, one must be sure to observe

---

1. Although these rests either hang from a line or sit on it as do their modern counterparts, the line of the staff to which they were attached was variable.

them very exactly: he who neglected this would disturb the concord and harmony of the music.

The first thing to do when one finds rests in a measure is to determine which voice they are in, then on what beat they occur, and finally what they are worth.

EXAMPLE

Of the Use of the Whole Rest

Of the Use of the Half Rest

Of the Use of the Quarter Rest

Of the Use of the Eighth Rest

Of the Use of the Sixteenth Rest

Although we have established the value of a whole rest as equal to a whole note and that of the half rest as equal to a half note, they both nevertheless change their value in accordance with the character of the pieces in which they are used, the practice being to use the whole rest to indicate a silence of a whole measure, and the half rest a silence of a half measure, no matter what the time signature. Thus in pieces whose measures are each worth more than a whole note, the whole rest is also worth more than a whole note and the half rest more than a half note. In those pieces whose measures are each worth less than a whole note, the whole rest is worth less than a whole note and the half rest less than a half note.

See above in the demonstration of the time signatures [ch. VIII, pp. 34-5] those which contain more than a whole note per measure and those which contain less.

Notice that the half rest is never used in triple time except in what is called double triple [$\frac{3}{2}$], where it is worth not half a measure, as in two- or four-beat measures, but a third of a measure, that is a half note, which is the value we gave it at first.

Since the above example of the use of rests only shows one voice in order to be more easily understood, we will give another example here that has several voices, as is standard for harpsichord pieces.

EXAMPLE OF THE USE OF RESTS IN HARPSICHORD PIECES

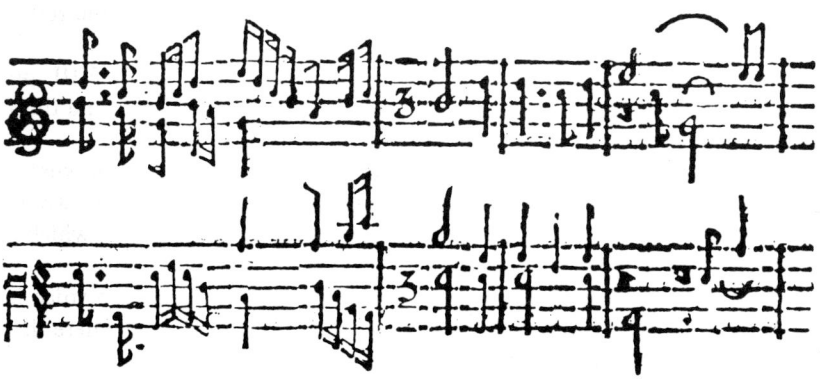

The most frequently used rests in harpsichord pieces are the quarter rest and the eighth rest; the other three are not found as often.

Rests are more frequent in the inner voices than in the treble or bass, and more frequent in the left hand than in the right.

Even though a half rest is equal in value to two quarter rests, it is never placed in a three-beat measure to notate a silence of two beats. Two quarter rests are always used.

The same is true of $\frac{3}{8}$ time, where a silence of two eighth notes is notated by two eighth rests, not by a quarter rest.

On the other hand, in a two- or four-beat measure, that is, measures which contain four quarter notes,[2] a silence of a half note or of two quarter notes is always indicated by a half rest and never by two quarter rests.

Two quarter rests in a three-beat measure indicate a silence of two beats only when they are side by side (see F, in the example below), for when

2. I.e. C, ¢, or 2.

they are one above the other (G), they only count as one, meaning only that the same one-beat silence occurs in two voices at once. In the same way several notes only count as one in relation to the beat when they must be played simultaneously.

The preceding rule is applicable to all rests and all notes which can enter into the construction of a harpsichord piece.

Rests may replace notes in a measure and both together make up the value demanded by the time signature. Thus two quarter rests and one quarter note are like three quarter notes, a half note and a half rest are like two half notes, etc.

CHAPTER XI

Concerning the Double Bar

(De la Double Barre)

Most harpsichord pieces are divided into two sections, and it is customary to play the first half twice in a row and then the second half twice also. It is in this way, as most everyone knows, that all songs [*chansons*] are divided. The midpoint of a piece is indicated by a double bar at the end of a measure with dots in the spaces between the lines.[1]

However, the double bar is not always placed at the end of a measure; it is sometimes halfway or three-quarters of the way through. No matter what beat of the measure it is on, it always marks the division of the piece.

The second half of a piece is called the *reprise*.[2] However, there are some pieces which are not divided simply in two but are separated into several *couplets*, such as chaconnes and passacailles. Each *couplet* is played twice and the end of every *couplet* is marked by a double bar.[3]

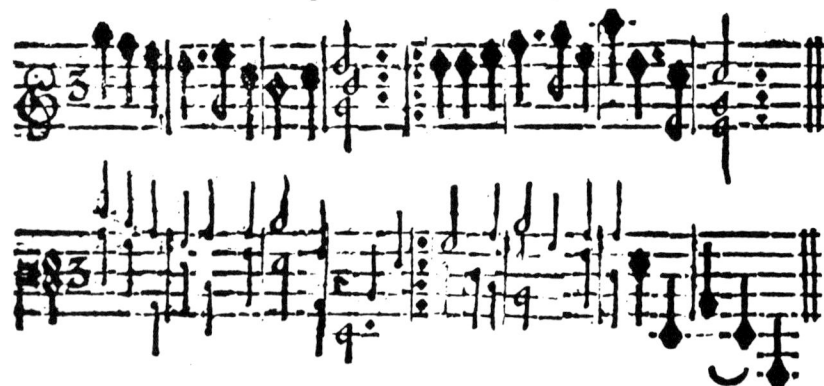

1. In this example, the double bar has been incorrectly printed. As the name indicates, it should actually be double, with a vertical line on both sides of the dots, i.e. ▦

For other examples of the double bar, see St Lambert's two pieces at the end of the book. Note that the usage of his day differs from the modern in that the final double bar of the piece sometimes lacks the dots indicating repetition, even though each section is to be played twice, as in the little example here and the menuet at the end of the book.

2. It is also usually labeled as such in the score. See the dance movements in the works of d'Anglebert, Lebègue, etc. Note the difference from modern usage which often refers to the first section of a binary composition as the 'first reprise'.

3. For an example of a passacaille notated in this way in which each four-measure *couplet* is repeated, see the passacaille in G minor in Jean Henry d'Anglebert's *Pièces de clavecin*, facsimile edition, pp. 51ff. The first page of this piece is reproduced in appendix A.

Couplets are also often written out completely, in which case there is no double bar at the end. Pieces without double bars are played from beginning to end without repeating anything, because whatever must be repeated has been written out twice. In composing this type of piece, composers write each *couplet* out twice when they want there to be a difference between the first and second times, as in the Chaconne from *Phaéton* and the Passacaille from *Armide*.[4] But if the second time is the same as the first, they don't bother to write out the *couplets* twice; they only indicate the repetition by a double bar. The double bar is to music what the word *bis* is to songs that are not notated.[5] For the word *bis* placed at the end of a line of verse means that it must be repeated, but when the repeating part is written out twice, the word *bis* is omitted.

4. Both these pieces, drawn from two of Lully's operas, may be found arranged for harpsichord in d'Anglebert's *Pièces de clavecin*, the Chaconne on pp. 29-33 and the Passacaille on pp. 63-6 of the facsimile edition. The first page of the Chaconne from *Phaéton* is reproduced in appendix A.

5. St Lambert probably means strophic songs in a light vein, such as the *vaudevilles* or *chansons à danser* popular in the seventeenth century, in which only the first verse is set to music. In subsequent verses, the word *bis* indicates a repetition of a particular line of text and its accompanying music.

CHAPTER XII

Concerning the Renvoy

In addition to the double bar, there is another sign that indicates repetition. This sign is called the *renvoy* and is made in this way: ⁎.

When this sign is found in a piece, it means that after having played the piece completely, that is the first and second halves twice each, it is also necessary to repeat the part from where the sign is marked to the end of the piece still another time. There is an example of this in the gavotte at the end of the book.[1]

[1]. This little repeated section is generally called the **petite reprise** and is very common in the dance pieces of the period.

CHAPTER XIII

Concerning the Direct and the Renvoy

(Du Guidon et du Renvoy)

The direct is a symbol made in this way: ⇌, which is placed in the score at the end of a staff in order to indicate by its position with what note the following staff begins. If the direct is placed on C at the end of the first staff, it means that the first note of the second staff will be C, etc. You may see examples of this in the pieces at the end of this book and in all music books. It is the head of the direct which marks the place, not its tail, which is drawn upwards in a random fashion. But remember that in harpsichord scores the second staff does not follow the first, but the first corresponds to the third. Thus the directs at the end of the first staff do not indicate the first notes of the second staff, but the first notes of the third, and for the same reason the directs on the second staff indicate the first notes of the fourth staff.

The direct is sometimes placed with the *renvoy* in order to indicate more precisely to which note to go when there is something to repeat in a piece aside from ordinary repetitions. There is an example in the gavotte [at the end of the book].

The abbreviations *Pre Fois, Sece Fois*, or *1e Fois, 2e Fois* [first time, second time], are often found at the end of the first and second halves of a piece. These words indicate the difference there must be between the first and second repetitions of the *couplet*, which is that the first time, the measure marked *1e Fois* is played plus all the following measures up to the one marked *2e Fois*, and the second time one skips the measure marked *1e Fois* and the ones following, and instead plays the ones marked *2e Fois*. The gavotte provides an example of this also.[1]

In operas, these differences are not indicated by these little words, but it is not a question of opera here. In this book I am teaching only harpsichord notation.

1. See also the d'Anglebert passacaille in appendix A.

CHAPTER XIV

Concerning Accidentals in General

(Des Feintes en Général)

Accidentals are symbols used in notation in order to change the natural pitch of certain notes to another pitch. There are three kinds of accidentals: the sharp, the flat, and the natural. The sharp raises the pitch of the note it accompanies. The flat on the other hand lowers it, and the natural raises it again. But each of these three requires its own explanation.

CHAPTER XV

Concerning the Sharp

(Du Dièze)

When a note is accompanied by a sharp, which is a symbol made in this way: ♯, the pitch of the note is changed and it is no longer found among the black keys of the keyboard,[1] despite what Chapter III teaches, but among the white keys in the following manner.

If a C is marked with a sharp in the score (see example A below), one must not express it by playing the black key C which corresponds to this note, but rather the neighboring white key C♯, which is dependent on it in a certain manner and replaces it on these occasions. This is the change the sharp makes in the note it accompanies. This is the use to which the white keys are put on the keyboard. This is why they have the same names as the black keys and why in my drawing of the keyboard [p. 18] I put these particular symbols on the keys.

Notice that the sharp is always placed in front of the note it serves (see A, in the example below), and never after it (as at B). Sometimes it is placed above (C), and sometimes below (D). Thus every time a sharp is found mixed in among several notes, it always refers to the note following it, and never the note preceding it. When it is above or below the note there is no ambiguity, but it is rarely placed in this manner and is almost always in front.

When a note in the score is accompanied by a sharp, and several notes on the same degree follow it without interruption (see E, below), the one sharp controls them all and they must all be played as if each were individually marked with a sharp. But if the following notes are interrupted by a note which changes degree (F), the sharp controls only those preceding

---

1. As mentioned in ch. II, the black and white keys on the harpsichord of St Lambert's day are the reverse of what they are on the piano.

the note that changes and not those following it, even though those that follow are on the same degree as the preceding ones (G).²

2. As the example shows, the bar line has nothing to do with whether an accidental is maintained or not. In measures 1-2 the F♯ continues across the bar because there is no change in pitch.

CHAPTER XVI

Concerning the Flat

(Du Bémol)

In the drawing of the keyboard presented earlier [p. 18], it may be noticed that the three white keys C, F, and G are characterized by the sharp, which is because in written music the three notes C, F, and G are more frequently accompanied by a sharp than the others. It sometimes happens, however, that other notes are sharpened also, but very rarely, and we reserve this for discussion in another place (see the Remarks).¹

The flat, like the sharp, has certain notes proper to itself and near which it is found more often than elsewhere, although it may occasionally accompany others. The notes commonly flattened are B and E. The symbol of the flat is ♭. In the drawing of the keyboard I have placed it on the two white keys E and B.²

2. St Lambert distinguishes between the notes that are sharpened and those that are flattened because of the prevailing preference for unequal temperaments. Although there were some proponents of equal temperament in the 17th century, the system generally referred to as mean-tone tuning was the norm. In equal temperament, the standard tuning system in Western music today, the octave is divided into twelve equal semitones and G♯, for example, has exactly the same pitch as A♭. In mean-tone tuning, the usable fifths are tempered but the thirds are tuned pure, or almost so, resulting in semitones of different sizes. Therefore G♯ and A♭ do not have the same pitch and the tuner of a keyboard instrument must choose between them. A number of different mean-tone temperaments were in use during the Baroque period. See J. Murray Barbour, *Tuning and Temperament: A Historical Survey* (East Lansing, 1953), and Mark Lindley, articles 'Mean-Tone' and 'Temperaments' in *The New*

1. Because this Remark discusses all three accidentals at length, it has been placed at the end of ch. XVII, pp. 64ff.

When a B accompanied by a flat is found in the score (see H, in the example below), one must not express it by playing the black key B which corresponds to this note, but rather the neighbouring white key B♭, as we said of the sharp.

The flat, like the sharp, is usually placed in front of the note it accompanies (as at H), sometimes above (I) or below (L), but never after.

The rules for sharps and flats are exactly the same: thus when there are several notes on the same degree without interruption after a note marked with a flat (see M, below), the flat controls them all and they must all be played as if each were individually marked with a flat. But if the following notes are interrupted by a note which changes degree (N), the flat controls only those preceding the note that changes and not those following, even though those that follow are on the same degree as the preceding ones (O).

When after a note marked with a sharp (see P, below) there is another on the same degree marked with a flat (Q), the flat then means that the sharp at P no longer controls the note Q, despite what the chapter on the sharp teaches, and that one must play the note Q and all those following on the same degree on the black key, not on the white key as the note P had been.

Grove Dictionary of Music and Musicians (London, 1980). For a 17th-century discussion of temperament, see Jean Denis, *Traité de l'accord de l'espinette* (Paris, 1650; reprinted by Da Capo Press, New York, 1969). For instructions on how to tune keyboard instruments in various tunings, including those prevalent in France in the 17th and 18th centuries, see Mark Lindley, 'Instructions for the clavier diversely tempered', *Early Music*, 5:1 (1977), pp. 18-23. For further relevant comments by St Lambert see the Remark in ch. XVIII, p. 67.

CHAPTER XVII

Concerning the Natural

(Du Béquarre)

The natural is a symbol made in this way: ♮, which serves on similar occasions to the one we just mentioned; that is when after a note marked with a flat (see R, in the example below) there is another on the same degree marked with a natural (as at S), the natural is there only to indicate that the flat on note R no longer controls the note S, despite what the chapter on the flat says, and that the note S and all those following on the same degree must be played on the black key and not on the white key, as the note R had been.

Sometimes in place of the natural there is a sharp (as at T), in which case the sharp has the same meaning as the natural.¹ [*]

* This is the place I reserved for discussion of [the theory of accidentals] and what is to be said on the subject concerning the sharp, the flat, and the natural. But we will treat them separately in order to avoid confusion.

Concerning the Sharp

The rule of the sharp is that every time it accompanies a note in the score, the note, no matter what it is, is played a semitone higher on the keyboard than it would be without the sharp. Thus when C is marked by a sharp in the score, instead of playing the black key C ☞

1. St Lambert's rules governing cancellation of accidentals, which are quite different from modern usage, may be summarized as follows:
 (1) accidentals are cancelled by a change in pitch but not by bar lines. For example, a sharpened F remains F♯ even across bar lines for as long as the pitch does not change, but as soon as another pitch is introduced, all subsequent Fs are natural;
 (2) a flat may be cancelled by either a sharp or a natural;
 (3) a sharp may be cancelled only by a flat. (Cf. the heading 'Concerning the Natural' in the Remark below, p. 66.)

which corresponds to this note, one plays the white key to its right, because the white key is a semitone higher. In the same way, when a D is marked by a sharp, one plays in place of the D the white key to its right, that is, the note usually called E-flat. But when it is an E that is marked by a sharp, one then plays F instead of the E because there is no white key to the right of E, and the F is only a semitone higher. But since I have not yet explained what a whole tone and semitone are, it is appropriate for me to do so here. Tone and semitone are the names of the intervals between the notes or keys in relation to the sounds they produce. The keys on the keyboard do not all produce the same sound: going from left to right the sound of the second note is higher than that of the first, the sound of the third note higher than that of the second, and so on for the rest until the end. The difference there is between the sound of one key and that of another is what is called whole tone or semitone. All the keys of the harpsichord, including white and black keys, are each a semitone apart: from C to the white key on its right is a semitone, from this white key to D is a semitone, from D to the following white key a semitone, from this white key to E a semitone, from E to F a semitone, and so on. But the black keys, compared only with each other, do not go up by semitone in this way. From C to D there is a whole tone, from D to E a whole tone, from E to F a semitone, from F to G a whole tone, from G to A a whole tone, from A to B a whole tone, and from B to C a semitone. Having explained this, it will be easy to understand what this rule means: every note that is accompanied by a sharp in the notation is played a semitone higher on the keyboard than it would be played otherwise.

The three notes C, F, and G are much more often accompanied by sharps than the others, and the keys to the right of these three notes have been given the names C♯, F♯, and G♯ because of the frequent use made of them as sharps. The rule requires that when a note replaces another as a sharp, it be called the sharp of the note it replaces.

Concerning the Flat

Every time that a note is accompanied by a flat in the score, no matter what the note is, it is played a semitone lower on the keyboard than it would be played otherwise. Thus when a B is marked with a flat in the score, instead of playing the black key B which corresponds to this note, one plays the white key to its left, because this white key is a semitone lower. When it is an A that is marked by a flat, one also plays the white key to its left, that is the note generally called G♯ and which on this occasion becomes A♭. But when it is an F that is marked, then one plays E in place of F, because there is no white key to the left of F, and because E is only a semitone lower.

The two notes B and E are much more often accompanied by flats than the others, and the keys to the left of these notes on the keyboard have been given the names B♭ and E♭ because of the frequent use made of these two white keys as flats. The rule requires, as we said about the sharp, that when a note replaces another as a flat, it be called the flat of the note it replaces.

The truth is, however, that the white keys have no name specifically their own, since the same keys that usually serve as sharps sometimes also serve as flats, and that those that often serve as flats sometimes also serve as sharps. In addition, if one wished to adhere to the letter of the law, not even the black keys would have fixed names, for since the same key is sometimes used as a natural, sometimes as a sharp, and sometimes as a flat, it seems there would be no reason to give it one name rather than another. However, it was indeed a good idea to give determined names to the white as well as to the black

☞ keys, because it is not reasonable always to vacillate, and it is definitely necessary to settle on one thing.

Through the choice of names that has been made for the keys of the harpsichord, each black note is found to have a white note dependent on it, either as a sharp or as a flat, excepting only D and A, which in ordinary usage have neither a sharp nor a flat named, but which in unusual circumstances each have a sharp and a flat like the others, for there is no key on the keyboard which is not, when the occasion demands, a sharp to its lower neighbor and a flat to its upper neighbor.

Concerning the Natural

The use of the natural is fairly similar to that of the sharp, for every time that a note is accompanied by a natural in the score, one plays it a semitone higher than it would be played otherwise. But it must be ☞ observed that the natural is only found in the score next to a note already controlled by a flat, so that it should not so much be said that it raises the note a semitone as that it returns it to its natural pitch, from which it had been diverted by the flat.

In the ordinary system of our music, B has a certain determined pitch, which is a tone higher than A and a semitone lower than C. But there are some pieces where it does not stay on this pitch. A flat marked next to the clefs[2] changes it and lowers it by a semitone. Thus the system is as new, since the B is no more than a semitone higher than the A, and it is on the other hand a whole tone lower than C. However, when in such a piece a natural appears for the purpose of raising one of these Bs a semitone, it only actually returns it to its natural pitch, from which it had been diverted by the flat next to the clefs.

2. I.e. a flat in the key signature.

CHAPTER XVIII

Concerning Transposed Pieces

(Des Pièces Transposées)

There are some pieces referred to as *transposed*, which are those whose clefs are accompanied by several sharps or flats, as shown in the following example.*¹

* One usually calls pieces transposed whose clefs are accompanied by sharps or flats, but it is incorrect to call them thus without any other distinction, for there are several which, despite having many flats or sharps, are not transposed at all and are, on the contrary, in very natural modes. Such are pieces in D, A, and B♭ major,² and several others. The only truly transposed modes are those whose chords do not have the usual intonation, as in several where the major thirds are more than major and others where the minor thirds are less than minor, in a word those modes where the intervals are either too large or too small. If I have called them all transposed, it is only to conform to common usage, plus the fact that the truth or falsity of the transposition of this kind of piece makes no difference to the rule in question in Chapter XVIII.³

1. In addition to this use of the word 'transposition', St Lambert discusses its more familiar meaning in his accompaniment treatise. See the *Nouveau traité de l'accompagnement du clavecin*, pp. 32-3.

2. It is unclear in the French whether or not St Lambert means the word 'major' to apply to the keys of D and A as well as B♭. In the accompaniment treatise, pp. 26-7, he states that when one speaks of a piece in D La Re or A Mi La without further distinction, the minor mode is to be understood.

3. The phenomenon St Lambert is discussing here is a result of using mean-tone tuning for the harpsichord rather than equal temperament. The 'very natural modes' he speaks of are the keys that are in tune in mean-tone tuning, such as C major, F major, G minor, etc. The 'truly transposed modes' are keys which are out of tune by virtue of including incorrectly tuned accidentals. For example, with a harpsichord whose white keys are tuned to C♯, E♭, F♯, G♯, and B♭, an F minor triad is out of tune, because the middle note is really a G♯, not an A♭. Since G♯ is lower in pitch than A♭ in the mean-tone system, this is one of the chords 'whose minor thirds are less than minor'. In a B major triad having what is really an E♭ in the middle, the major third is too large. It is, of course, possible to retune the accidentals in order to accommodate some of these problem chords, depending on what keys one wishes to play in. But it is also true that the colorings that certain chords and keys acquired on account of unequal tunings were highly appreciated by many musicians.

EXAMPLE OF TRANSPOSITIONS

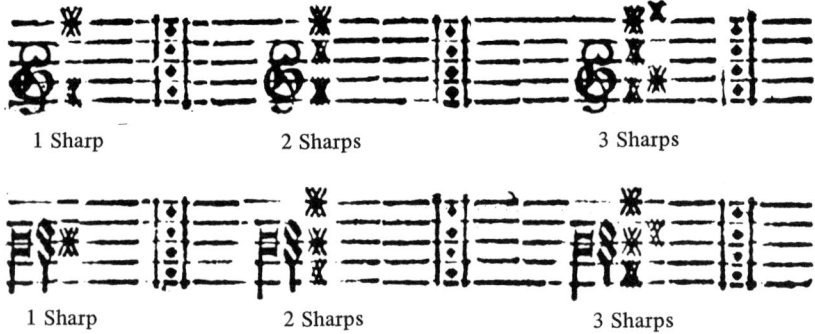

Transposition by Sharp

1 Sharp   2 Sharps   3 Sharps

1 Sharp   2 Sharps   3 Sharps

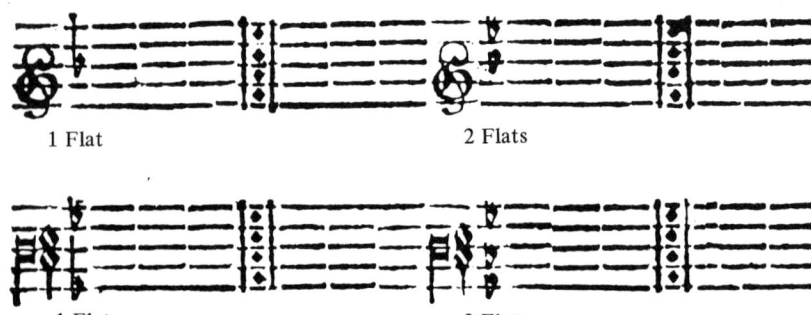

Transposition by Flat

1 Flat   2 Flats

1 Flat   2 Flats

Although the rules concerning the sharp and flat are the same, and that which may be said of one is applicable to the other, we will treat them separately in order to avoid any confusion arising from the double application of the rules. Starting with transposition by sharp, we will say that there are seven degrees of transposition, that is, that the clefs may be accompanied by one, two, three, or up to seven sharps, but it is rare for there to be more than three.

Two sharps near the clefs are considered as one when they are both placed on degrees having the same name, as can be seen in the example above.

When there is only one sharp, it is always on F. When there are two, one is on F, the other on C, and when there are three they are on F, C, and G. See the example above.

The sharps placed next to the clefs control the scale degrees on which they are placed, that is to say, if there is a sharp on F placed next to the clefs, all the notes of this degree must be played as if each one were individually marked with a sharp. It is the same for C and G and all the degrees that can be controlled by a sharp.

When the degree to be controlled by a sharp is found twice within the space of the five lines due to the position of the clef, as for example if there are two Fs, two Cs, or two Gs, then sharps are placed on both of these degrees; and two sharps of this type count for one, as I said, because they are on two degrees which have the same name.

But when the degree to be controlled by a sharp is only found once within the five lines, then only one sharp is placed next to the clef. See the example above.

The sharp next to the clef controls both the notes of its own degree and all those in the piece which have the same name. Thus, if it is on F, it controls both the Fs of its own degree and all the notes in the piece that are called F, whether they are on that exact degree or on another. It has the same effect on the degrees C and G when it is there, and generally speaking on all degrees where it may be placed.

If in a piece transposed by sharp it happens that one of the notes controlled by the sharps is marked with a flat, the flat in this case means that this particular note is no longer controlled by the sharp, and that it must be played as if the piece were not transposed, this note and all others following it without interruption on the same degree, in conformity to the last rule in the chapter on flats.

In a non-transposed piece, it may happen by chance that one or several notes marked by sharps are found right next to the clef, and in the absence of any warning one could take the piece to be transposed. However, one must realize that a piece is only transposed when all the clefs are accompanied by sharps and when these sharps are always on the same degrees. So much for transposition by sharp. Now we come to transposition by flat.

Transposition by flat has seven different degrees, just as the one we discussed above does, that is to say that the clefs may be accompanied by up to seven flats, but usually there are no more than two.

One speaks of two flats when they are on degrees having different names; when they are on pitches having the same name they count only as one. See the example above.

When there is only one flat, it is always on B. When there are two, one is on B, the other on E. See the example above.

If the degree to be controlled by a flat is found twice within the space of the five lines due to the position of the clef, then the flat is indicated twice, once on the upper pitch and again on the lower. But if the degree to be controlled by a flat is only found once, then only one flat is used. See the example above.

A flat next to the clef controls both the notes on the degree it occupies and all those in the piece that have the same name. Thus when there is a flat on B next to the clefs, the Bs on the same degree and all the Bs in the piece must be played as if each one were individually marked by a flat.

When in a piece transposed by flat it happens that one of the notes controlled by a flat is marked with a natural or a sharp, the natural or the sharp in this case means that the note is no longer governed by the flat and that it must be played as if the piece were not transposed, this note and all others following it without interruption on the same degree, in conformity to what the chapter on the natural teaches.

Just as a piece is only transposed by sharp when all the clefs are accompanied by sharps, placed on the same degrees for each clef, so is a piece only transposed by flat when all the clefs are accompanied by flats, placed on the same degrees for each clef. Thus be careful not to assume that a piece is transposed if chance has placed a few notes marked by a flat next to one of the two clefs. Remember that there is no transposition unless there are flats on the same degrees for every clef.

CHAPTER XIX

Concerning the Position of the Fingers[1]

(De la Position des Doigts)

There is nothing freer in playing the harpsichord than the position of the fingers. Each person seeks in it only his own convenience and gracefulness. But since there are some occasions when all those who play use their fingers in the same way, because it has been recognized that this is what is the most appropriate, a kind of rule has been established that one is almost obliged to follow and to which beginners at least cannot avoid submitting themselves.

This rule has less to do with those passages in which the hand has only one note to play at a time than those in which it has more than one.

Several notes played at the same time with only one hand are called a *chord* in harpsichord terminology.*[2] There are chords of two, three, and four notes. A two-note chord may be a third, a fourth, a fifth, a sixth, or an octave. A third is a chord extending three steps, a fourth a chord which occupies four steps, a fifth one that goes to five, and so on for the rest, as the examples below will demonstrate.

A three-note chord may be composed of two thirds, or a third and a fourth, or a fifth and a fourth.

A four-note chord is usually only composed of two thirds and a fourth. Sometimes it has three thirds, but less often.

Chords are found more frequently in the bass than in the treble, but they are not played with the same fingers in the right hand as in the left.

☞ is only given to those played with a single hand, either the right or the left.

---

*   A chord is the product of several sounds played simultaneously which, through their conjunction, form an agreeable consonance. However, when one says the product of several sounds, that can mean two as well as four or six. In that sense there is no harpsichord piece that is not made up of chords, since all of them have at least two voices, and every time these two voices strike together, they form a chord. However, this is not called a chord in harpsichord terminology: that name

1. In addition to this chapter, information about fingering may be found in ch. XXI, 'Concerning the *Tremblement*', and in the first paragraph of the final Remarks, p. 99. There are also two fully fingered pieces of St Lambert's composition at the end of the book.

2. In the original there is no reference to the Remarks made in this place, but the eleventh Remark at the back of the book clearly belongs here. Further on in this same chapter, St Lambert says 'See the Remarks' when there is none for that place. There appears to have been simply a mistake in placing the reference.

The Position of the Fingers

In harpsichord terminology, the thumb on each hand is referred to as the first finger, the next one the second, the middle one the third, the following one the fourth, and the little one the fifth.

EXAMPLE OR DEMONSTRATION OF THE NATURE OF CHORDS, AND OF THE FINGERS THAT MUST BE USED TO PLAY THEM[3]

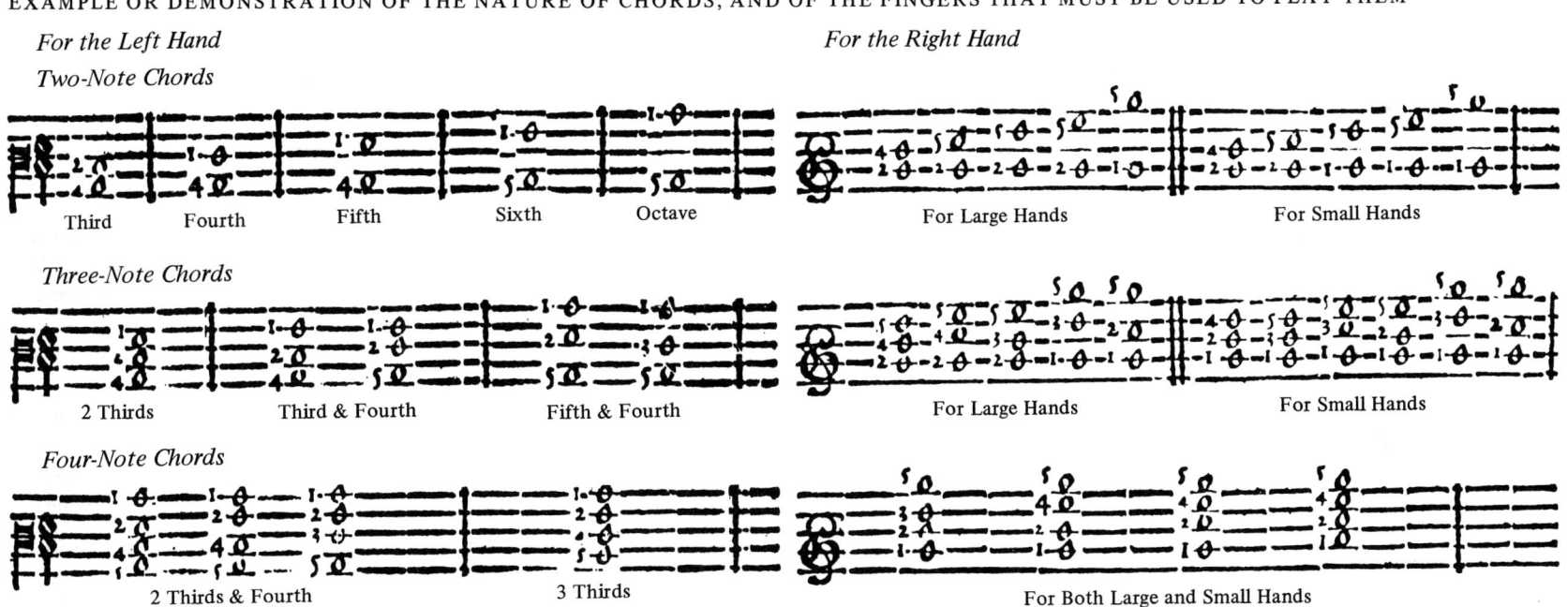

3. A transcription into modern clefs of St Lambert's fingering examples may be found at the end of appendix C, pp. 126-7.

When there is an accidental, that is, a sharp or a flat on the upper note of some chords in the left hand and on the lower note of others in the right hand, the position of the fingers is changed.

Left hand, large or small

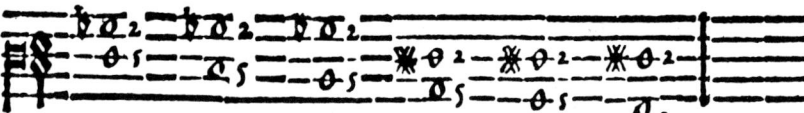

Left hand, large or small

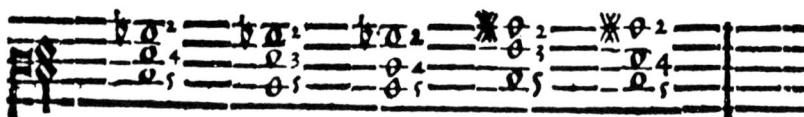

Right hand, large or small

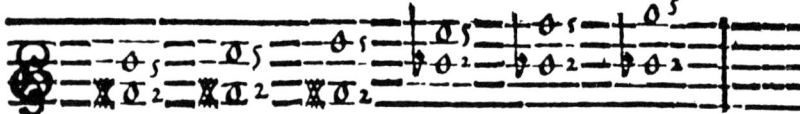

Right hand, large or small

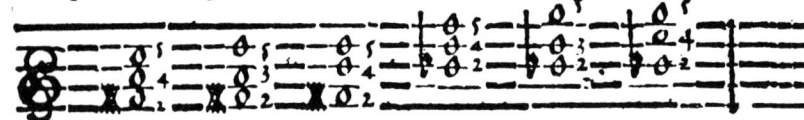

But when the upper and lower notes of a chord each have an accidental, they are played in the manner we taught first, that is, as if there were no accidental at all.

When there are accidentals in the middle of a chord, nothing is changed in the position of the fingers.

There are some passages which, without being chords, become so by the way in which the notes are arranged, and by the rule which obliges one to hold some down until others are played, as was taught in the chapter on the slur [pp. 29ff]. In these instances the position of the fingers is the same as for chords.[4]

For the Left Hand

For the Right Hand

4. The examples do show identical fingerings for broken chords as for simultaneously played chords with one exception, the interval of a 6th in the left hand. The use of 4-1 here may be due to the fact that the 6th is minor and thus slightly smaller than the major sixth fingered 5-1, but also probably reflects the frequent practice of the period of avoiding the use of the fifth finger on a white (black on the piano) key.

I will not multiply these examples further: it would be useless. Good sense alone is sufficient to recognize these passages when they occur in pieces and to make it clear that they may appear in as many ways as there are different types of chords.[5]

In regard to passages in which the hand has only one note to play at a time, there is only one occasion when the fingers are subjected to a rule: this is when there are many notes in a row which ascend or descend by

5. Certain general patterns in the fingering of chords, simultaneous or broken, may be observed in St Lambert's examples:
(1) the same fingers are assigned different functions in the right hand and in the left;
(2) there is a dendency to avoid the thumb in the right hand and the fifth finger in the left hand when the size of the interval permits. E.g. a fourth in the right hand is fingered 2-5, in the left 4-1, and a G major triad is fingered 2-4-5 in the right hand and 4-2-1 in the left;
(3) both hands avoid placing the thumb on a white key (black on the piano) when at all possible. This prohibition overrides the tendency to avoid the fifth finger in the left hand and means that where an accidental occurs on the top note of bass chords, the fingering in the two hands are now mirror images of each other;

(4) there is also a tendency to avoid using 5 on a white key, at least in the left hand. Cf. the examples of broken chords in the left hand and the left-hand part in St Lambert's gavotte at the end of the book. There are unfortunately no relevant right-hand examples given. This avoidance of 1 and 5 on white keys follows from the inherent inequality in length between the outer two and inner three fingers.

The other principal sources for keyboard fingerings from late 17th- and early 18th-century France are the preface to Guillaume-Gabriel Nivers's [*Premier*] *Livre d'orgue* (1665) (see appendix B) and *L'Art de toucher le clavecin* of François Couperin (1717). In addition there are occasional fingerings marked in keyboard pieces, as in André Raison's two *Livres d'orgue* (1688 and 1714), and Jean-François Dandrieu's *Pièces de clavecin courtes et faciles* (included in Dandrieu, *Trois livres de clavecin de jeunesse*, ed. Brigitte François-Sappey, Paris, 1975). Rameau also includes some remarks regarding fingering in the essay. 'De la méchanique des doigts sur le clavier' attached to his *Pièces de clavecin* of 1724.

Many of Nivers's chord fingerings are identical to St Lambert's, although he gives more examples using the thumb in the right hand. Most of Couperin's extensive examples are actual passages from his first and second books of harpsichord pieces; he gives no isolated chord fingerings as do Nivers and St Lambert. Study of his examples reveals that while he does not avoid using the fifth finger on a white key, he rarely places the thumb there and even changes the fingering of sequential figures to avoid it, as may be seen in the following passage from *La Zénobie* (Book II) (*L'Art de toucher le clavecin*, ed. Anna Linde (Leipzig, 1933), p. 38).

Couperin also uses the same fingering as St Lambert for first inversion triads in the right hand, a common cadential chord (*ibid.*, p. 37).

step without interruption. In this case one uses the fingerings marked in the following example.⁶

Right Hand

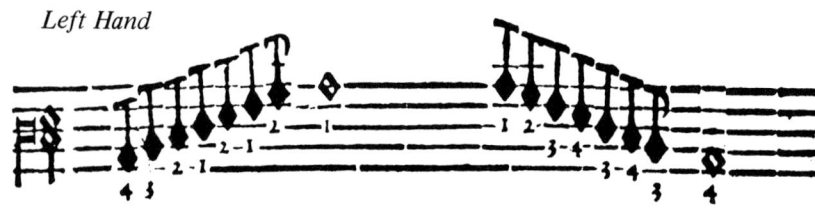

Left Hand

6. Note the changes in fingerings between hands and between ascending and descending passages. Identical fingerings of stepwise passages may be found in the works of other French keyboard players both before and after St Lambert. Cf. Nivers and François Couperin. Already in Couperin, however, there are indications of a shift toward the use of consecutive fingerings in certain types of passages, and Rameau in his *Pièces de clavecin* of 1724 appears to have abandoned paired fingerings.

In all other occasions one uses the fingers as one deems appropriate [see the Remarks],⁷ either well or badly depending on whether one has judgment and taste in the matter. The convenience of the player is the first rule that must be followed; gracefulness is the second.⁸ The latter consists of holding the hands straight on the keyboard, that is to say not bending them too far up or down,⁹ of having the fingers curved and all arranged at the same level based on the length of the thumb, of having the wrist at the same height as the elbow, which depends on the type of seat one takes, and of not raising the fingers too high while playing and not pressing too hard on the keys.¹⁰

7. The relevant passage is to be found as the second part of a Remark attached to ch. XXI, 'Concerning the *Tremblement*', p. 77. It actually refers to diminutions and suggests the use of the thumb and first finger for descending stepwise figures in the right hand.

8. Cf. the Final Remarks, p. 100, where St Lambert says that the basic principle of fingering is to choose fingers that make the hand move the least.

9. 'Celle-cy consiste à tenir ses mains droites sur le Clavier; c'est-à-dire, ne penchant ny en dedans ny en dehors.'

The phrase 'ne penchant ny en dedans ny en dehors' is somewhat ambiguous, but other keyboard manuals have injunctions against holding the wrist higher or lower than the hands, which is probably what St Lambert means. Cf. Jean Denis, *Traité de l'accord de l'espinette* (1650), p. 37, who says that the wrist should be level with the hands, not higher or lower. Cf. also François Couperin, *L'Art*, Linde edn, pp. 10-11, who says that elbows, wrists, and fingers should all be on the same level.

10. Cf. Fr. Couperin, who is even more emphatic on this point: 'Delicacy of touch depends also on holding the fingers as close to the keys as possible' (*L'Art*, Linde edn, p. 12).

CHAPTER XX

Concerning Agréments[1] in General

If the choice of fingers in playing the harpsichord is arbitrary, the choice of *agréments* is no less so. Good taste is the only rule that must be followed. However, there are some *agréments* which are virtually essential to pieces[2] and which are difficult to do without. The most important of these is the *tremblement*; the others are the *pincé*, the *arpégé*, and the *coulé*.[3] But even though those which we will discuss after these first four are neither as necessary nor as frequently used, they nevertheless give a great deal of grace to pieces, and it would be a mistake to neglect them.

---

1. The plethora of names and variants in the *agréments* found in French music of the 17th and 18th centuries is a constant source of confusion and controversy for students of the period. Many of the ornaments given by St Lambert have different names or are performed differently in the works of other writers. For a thorough discussion of the different types of *agréments* and the names they are given in early sources, see Putnam C. Aldrich, 'The principal *agréments* of the seventeenth and eighteenth centuries: a study in musical ornamentation' (Ph.D. dissertation, Harvard University, 1942); and Frederick Neumann, *Ornamentation in Baroque and Post-Baroque Music* (Princeton, 1978).

2. Here and elsewhere the word 'pieces' means solo harpsichord pieces, not those in which the harpsichord plays continuo.

3. Cf. ch. XXIV, where St Lambert says that the *port de voix* is one of the more important *agréments*.

CHAPTER XXI

Concerning the Tremblement

The *tremblement* is an agitation of two keys struck alternately as equally and as quickly as possible.[1] It is indicated in the notation by a symbol made in this way: ⌇,[2] placed above or below the note to be trilled, as is shown in the example below. The symbol indicating the *tremblement* is also called the *tremblement* in ordinary usage, just as all the other symbols indicating *agréments* bear the name of the *agréments* that they designate.

Since the *tremblement* is an alternate striking of two notes or keys, one must borrow a second note in order to play it, because the *tremblement* is marked on only one note. The borrowed note is always the upper neighbor of the one marked by the *tremblement*. For example, if the note C is marked, one borrows the note D and strikes the two notes D and C alternately and rapidly.

The *tremblement* is begun with the borrowed note and ends with the main note.

Since the keys that one strikes are adjacent to each other, it is also necessary for the fingers striking them to be adjacent.

In the right hand, the fingers used for *tremblements* are the third and second or the fourth and third, and for the left hand the first and second or the second and third*.[3]

* *Remark on the choice of fingers for tremblements and diminutions*: Masters of the harpsichord have established the practice of only playing *tremblements* with the fingers indicated in this chapter, but when they made this rule they assuredly did not give it enough thought. They should have considered that it is impossible to accustom the fingers to too much agility and that nothing makes them more supple than the *tremblement*. Thus they should have established the practice of doing *tremblements* with all the fingers of each hand, even with the little finger and the thumb; at least this is the advice I will give to those who do me the honor of referring to me on the subject, and I am persuaded that they will find it to their advantage. For if one examines all the capable masters in Paris, one will discover that those who distinguish themselves the most by beauty of touch and sureness ☞

---

1. Cf. St Lambert's qualification of this definition below, p. 77.
2. This symbol is notated sideways in the original text from the way it appears in all the examples.

3. Notice that St Lambert always gives fingerings for the *tremblements* in the order the fingers are played, that is starting with the upper note and finger.
   Fr. Couperin and Nivers give the same fingerings for *tremblements* as St Lambert, but Nivers says that 4-3 in the right hand and 1-2 in the left are more frequently used (Nivers, *Premier livre d'orgue* (1665), preface, and Fr. Couperin, *L'Art*, Linde edn, p. 17).

Beginners have much more difficulty in striking the *tremblement* with the fourth and third fingers of the right hand than with the third and second, just as with the left hand they strike the *tremblement* better with the second and third fingers than with the first and second. As a result, they usually neglect the fingers that give them difficulty and only use those they can move easily. But it is necessary to exercise all the fingers equally, because there are some occasions when one is obliged to play a *tremblement* with these difficult fingers, just as there are others when one

☞ of execution are those who make use of all their fingers equally well, by having accustomed themselves early to exercising them all equally.⁴

For Diminutions

A diminution is a passage of several notes which must go very fast, as for example sixteenth notes. However, when there is a diminution to play in the right hand, if the notes are always descending, the practice is to use the second and third fingers alternately, as I indicated in the chapter on the position of the fingers [ch. XIX, p. 74]. But I will add here that this practice does not seem to me well founded and that the thumb and the second finger would be more appropriate for this kind of passage than the second and third fingers, because since the thumb is shorter than the other fingers, it is easier to draw it from under the third when the right hand descends with the latter two. The same reason one has for using the thumb in ascending diminutions in the left hand should induce one to use it in descending diminutions in the right hand as well.

4. St Lambert is not necessarily recommending that his readers use these fingerings for *tremblements* in solo pieces, but that they practice them in order to acquire greater agility in the weaker fingers. In his own two pieces at the end of this book he uses only the standard fingerings for *tremblements*.

can avoid them. However, we will not discuss these occasions here, there being no method to determine them precisely, but only good sense which can judge them.

The value of the note on which the *tremblement* is marked determines the duration of the striking [of the two alternating notes]. It is longer on a whole note than on a half note, and longer on a half note than on a quarter note, etc.

When the *tremblement* must be long, it is more beautiful to strike it slowly at first, and to speed it up only at the end,⁵ but when it is short it must always be quick.⁶

The fingers that play the *tremblement* must not stay on both the keys they have struck when finishing the ornament. The finger playing the borrowed note must remain in the air, and the one playing the main note must stay on the key for as long as the value of the note permits. (I use the two words 'note' and 'key' to mean the same thing when speaking of *agréments*.)

DEMONSTRATION OF THE *TREMBLEMENTS*

Right Hand   *Left Hand*

5. This important qualification of St Lambert's initial categorical definition of a *tremblement* as a rapid and equal alternation of two notes is a good example of his pedagogical principles in action. Cf. his definition of a good teacher in the Foreword: 'He teaches a general rule as if it were without exception, waiting for an occasion to produce this exception before speaking about it . . . '
6. Cf. Fr. Couperin, who says that *tremblements* must begin more slowly than they end but that the gradation must be imperceptible (*L'Art*, Linde edn, p. 17).

AS PLAYED

When there are other notes to play at the same time as the trilled note, either with the hand playing the *tremblement* or with the other, one must strike these other notes exactly when beginning the *tremblement*, that is, as soon as one plays the borrowed note used to make the *tremblement* for the first time.[7]

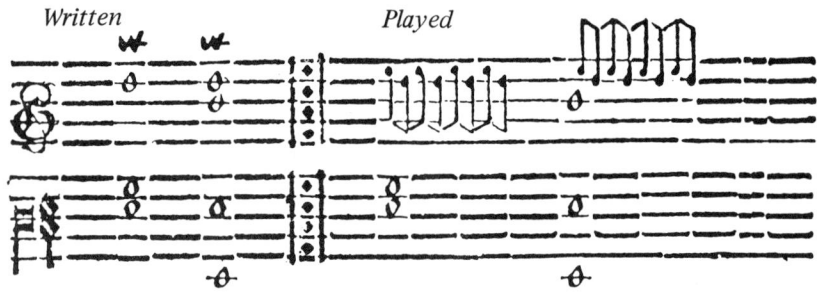

7. From this statement it is clear that St Lambert's *tremblement* should start with the upper note squarely on the beat. On this point there is remarkable agreement among the keyboard composers of the late 17th century: their ornament tables all show this same pattern for the *tremblement*, or *cadence*, as it was also called. Cf. Nivers (1665), Chambonnières (1670), Lebègue (1677), Raison (1688), d'Anglebert (1689), Chaumont (1696), Dieupart (*c.* 1702), and Le Roux (1705).

When the note marked by a *tremblement* is preceded or followed in the score by a note a step higher marked by an accidental, either a sharp or a flat, it is necessary to borrow this altered upper neighbor on the keyboard in order to play the *tremblement*.[8]

8. There are two misprints in these examples. In the second measure of the first example, the *tremblement* should be marked above the third note, not the second. In the third measure of the second example, the first note is different in the two versions.

St Lambert never discusses how to end a *tremblement*, but these examples offer some information. Both *tremblements* in the first example and the final one in the second are cadential and all three have a stop on the main note (a *point d'arrêt*, to use Fr. Couperin's term) before the termination. The *tremblement* in the first measure of the second example is on a note in the middle of a phrase and continues for the full value of the note. The note values of the written-out versions are, of course, approximate, and these examples should not be taken as the only ways to terminate trills. Cf. St Lambert's comments at the end of ch. XXVIII, 'Concerning the *Aspiration*' (pp. 98ff) regarding the freedom of the performer in the use of *agréments*.

Written

Played

Even if there is a note or two between the altered note and the *tremblement* a step lower which follows or precedes it (see notes marked A, B, C, and D below), one nevertheless borrows the accidental in playing the *tremblement*, because the ear cannot accept the *tremblement* without this altered note just a moment before or after hearing [this accidental].⁹

The *tremblement* is also played with the accidental independently of what precedes or follows it when the sign indicating a *tremblement* is accompanied by an accidental.

9. Note that this use of accidentals differs from modern practice in that accidentals can be retroactive and the bar line is not a factor. The harmonic context determines the upper note of the *tremblement*.

Written   *Played*

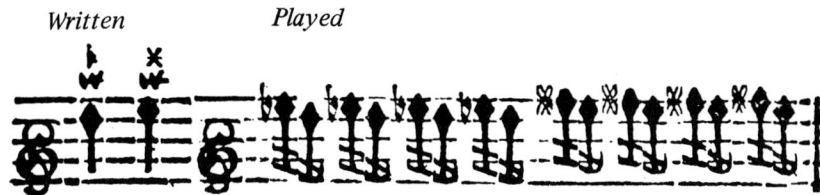

It is not common for the sign marking a *tremblement* to include an accidental, but when that happens it is more likely to be a flat than a sharp.

In transposed pieces,¹⁰ all the *tremblements* are played with an accidental when they are on notes a step lower than those controlled by accidentals. Thus in a piece transposed by a sharp, a *tremblement* on E is made to F♯, not to F♮, because since the Fs are controlled by a sharp, every time one plays an F, either as an essential note or as a borrowed note, one must play F♯. The same is true in pieces transposed by flat: a *tremblement* on A is made to B♭ and not to B♮, because the Bs are controlled by the flat.

There is one exception to this rule, and that happens when the *tremblement* is preceded or followed by a note a step higher marked by an accidental that cancels the first accidental and makes the note natural. For example, when in a piece transposed by sharp there is an F marked with a flat, which in this case cancels the sharp in accordance with what we said in Chapter XVIII, if this F is followed or preceded by an E that must be trilled, then the *tremblement* on this E will be made to F♮ and not to F♯, since for the moment the F is no longer controlled by the sharp.

For the same reason, if in pieces transposed by flat there is a sharp or natural which cancels the flat, in accordance with Chapter XVIII, and if

10. I.e. pieces with sharps or flats in the key signature; see ch. XVIII.

this natural is preceded or followed by a note a step lower marked with a *tremblement*, in this case it will be as if the piece were not transposed, because the transposition is cancelled for the moment.

If there happened to be a note or two between the natural that cancels the transposition and the note to be trilled, one would still play the *tremblement* in the way we just said, as in the preceding example.[11]

In any piece, transposed or not, the *tremblement* on a note marked with an accidental is always made to its natural neighbor and not to a neighbor that is altered like itself. For example, a *tremblement* on F♯ is made to G♮ and not to G♯, C♯ to D♮, and so on.

There is one instance in which a *tremblement* on F♯ is made to G♯, and that is when G is also controlled by a sharp through some one of the rules we discussed earlier.

11. I.e. the verbal examples given in the two preceding paragraphs.

In pieces in which C, F, and G are controlled by sharps, as in the above example, the *tremblement* on F♯ must always be made to G♯, unless the *tremblement* on F is preceded or followed by a G made natural for a moment, as we have repeated so many times in the preceding rules.

But in order to clarify what has just been said for the sake of the reader, I am going to reduce the substance of it to two rules which will include all that can be taught on the subject:

1. The *tremblement*, in that which concerns the borrowed note, is always regulated by the nature of the upper neighboring note. If by the laws of the mode that note is a sharp, then the *tremblement* is made to a sharp. If it is a flat, the *tremblement* is made to a flat, and if it is natural, the *tremblement* is played with a natural key. This is the important and infallible rule concerning the *tremblement*. The second is no less important, even though it is only the exception to this first general rule.

2. In any possible instance either in pieces transposed by flat or sharp or in non-transposed pieces, as far as the borrowed note is concerned the *tremblement* is always regulated according to the note preceding or following it in the score, provided that this note is a step higher than the one to be trilled.[12]

It is sufficient to understand these two rules in order to know everything concerning the *tremblement*, but be aware that the first is the general rule, the second the individual rule and the exception to the general one.

I have dwelt upon the rules for the *tremblement* at length because a

12. These two rules may be paraphrased as follows:
(1) The upper neighbor borrowed in order to play a *tremblement* should properly be a note found in the scale established by the key signature of the piece.
(2) If the upper neighbor to the *tremblement* is altered when it is found in close proximity to the *tremblement*, then the altered note is used in playing the ornament, not the pitch indicated by the key signature.

clear explanation of this *agrément* makes an understanding of the others much easier.

The other *agréments* are like the *tremblement* in that they add to the notes marked for that purpose other notes that are not written in the score. Thus it will be sufficient to indicate here all the signs that signify *agréments* and to explain in notes how they must be performed. But before starting this enumeration, I will first speak of the different kinds of *tremblements* that one can do.

Monsieur d'Anglebert distinguishes five *tremblements* which are explained along with other *agréments* of his invention in the book of pieces he gave to the public. I have collected all these *agréments* here, as well as those of the other masters who have had their works engraved.[13] Here are the five *tremblements* of M. d'Anglebert. First there is the *tremblement simple*, for which we gave the rules at the beginning of the chapter, and then the *tremblement appuyé*, which consists of playing the borrowed note once before starting the *tremblement*. He calls the third and fourth ones *cadences* and gives the fifth the compound name of *tremblement et pincé*.

DEMONSTRATION OF THE SYMBOLS THAT INDICATE THE DIFFERENT KINDS OF *TREMBLEMENTS* ACCORDING TO M. D'ANGLEBERT

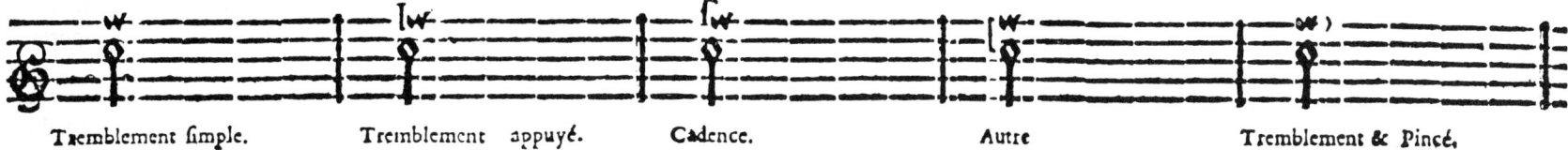

MANNER OF PLAYING THESE DIFFERENT *TREMBLEMENTS*[14]

---

13. The ornament tables of the keyboard composers mentioned by St Lambert may be found in appendix B.

14. In the realization of the *tremblement appuyé* below, the tie between the first two Ds indicated in d'Anglebert's table has been omitted. This could well be a printing error, since St Lambert's stated purpose is to reproduce d'Anglebert's ornaments, but given St Lambert's verbal definition of the *tremblement appuyé*, the omission may have been deliberate.

M. Nivers mentions three different *tremblements*. He calls the first one *agrément*, the second *cadence*, and the third *double cadence*. He defines and expresses them in the following manner.

DEMONSTRATION OF THE *TREMBLEMENTS* ACCORDING TO M. NIVERS[15]

MANNER OF PLAYING THEM

The *tremblement* that M. Nivers calls the *agrément* is the same as that which the other masters call the *pincé*, as will be seen later, except that he starts it on the borrowed note and the others start it on the main note.[16]

What he calls the *double cadence* is the same *agrément* as what M. d'Anglebert calls the *tremblement et pincé*. Thus there is no difference between the *agréments* of these two masters other than their names and the manner of indicating them on paper.

M. de Chambonnières and M. Lebègue recognize only one type of *tremblement*,[17] which is the one we spoke of first and which M. d'Anglebert calls *simple*. They both indicate it by the sign ⁀.

---

15. Nivers's ornament symbols are actually somewhat different from St Lambert's version of them. See his table in appendix B.

16. See ch. XXIII, 'Concerning the *Pincé*', p. 84.

17. Chambonnières calls it *cadence*, Lebègue *cadence ou tremblement*.

CHAPTER XXII

Concerning the Double Cadence

Since many people call the *tremblement* a *cadence*, I will place the *double cadence* following this first *agrément*, even though I had originally intended to put this chapter elsewhere.

The *double cadence* is indicated and performed in the following manner.

The *double cadence* is usually followed by a *tremblement*.

But when the *tremblement* does not follow, it is done another way.

Another Example On a Third   *Played*[1]

1. The upper note in the realization of this ornament has been displaced by a third. As seen in d'Anglebert's table, it should actually be:

Note that the turning figure proper (C-B-A-B) is rhythmically offset.

83

The last two ways are the invention of M. d'Anglebert, but the first is used by everyone and was, I believe, invented by M. de Chambonnières.²

2. The first of St Lambert's *doubles cadences* is the only one appearing in Chambonnières's brief ornament table. The configuration of the combined *double cadence* and *tremblement* is taken from d'Anglebert. In their ornament tables (see appendix B) both Chambonnières and d'Anglebert give the *double cadence* a more precise, although differing, rhythmic realization. Nivers and Lebègue do not discuss this ornament.

These examples of the *double cadence* point up an interesting anomaly in both St Lambert and d'Anglebert: all the *doubles cadences* involve a turning figure over the interval of a third, but in the first two examples, the ornament descends a third from the main note, whereas in the third and fourth examples the main note is the center of the turn. In this case the differing melodic functions of the ornaments rather than their names serve to distinguish them.

CHAPTER XXIII

Concerning the Pincé

M. d'Anglebert distinguishes three types of *pincé*, which he indicates by these signs:

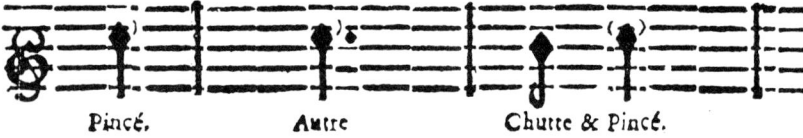

He expresses them in this manner:

In the *agrément* called here *chute et pincé*, the first note is not essential.¹ It is there simply to show that this *agrément* is only done when the note preceding it is a step lower. The *chute et pincé* is the same thing as that which M. Nivers simply calls the *agrément*.²

1. That is, the written eighth note is not part of the ornament.
2. In ch. XXI, St Lambert had said that 'the *tremblement* that M. Nivers calls the *agrément* is the same as what other masters call the *pincé*, except that he starts it on the borrowed note and the others start it on the main note' (p. 82). In his *Premier livre d'orgue* of 1690, Gilles Jullien gives this same ornament but calls it *agrément ou pincement*, thus providing a link in the nomenclature between Nivers and the other composers cited by St Lambert.

Note that the rhythm of the first two *pincés* is copied accurately from d'Angle-

It must be said of these first two *pincés* in the preceding example that the first, being shorter and less figured than the second, is more appropriate to short notes, and the second to long notes.[3]

M. de Chambonnières and M. Lebègue speak of only one kind of *pincé*, which they both indicate by the mark ✦ and express as the following example shows.[4]

bert's table but that the third is not. D'Anglebert's realization of the *chute et pincé* is:

The rhythmic realization of all these *pincés* shows them beginning on the beat.

See the end of the following chapter, 'Concerning the *Port de Voix*', for comments regarding the appropriate use of the *pincé*.

3. Note that there is no difference in the symbols for these two *pincés*. The choice is dependent on the musical context and the taste of the performer.

4. More accurately their symbol is ₩ and both call this ornament *pincement*. At the end of the Foreword, p. 7, St Lambert says that he prefers this symbol for the *pincé* to d'Anglebert's (ɼ'), although in his musical examples he always uses the latter.

CHAPTER XXIV

Concerning the Port de Voix

The *port de voix* is one of the more important *agréments* for the harpsichord, even though not all the masters mention it.[1] M. d'Anglebert acknowledges two types, one ascending, the other descending. He indicates and expresses them as demonstrated in the following example.

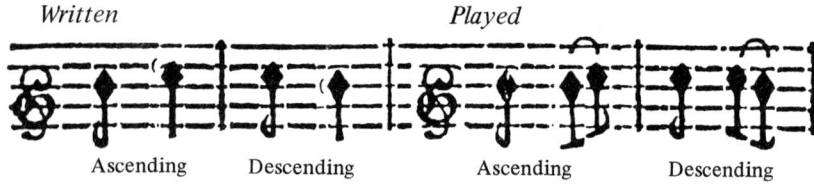

The pen stroke ⌒ drawn above the notes in the realization of the *port de voix* is a slur, which means that it is necessary to run those notes together [*couler ces Notes-là*], that is to say that one must not raise the fingers while playing them, but wait until the second of the two notes is played before raising the finger that played the first one.[2]

The rule of the *port de voix* is that one must play the note preceding the one bearing the ornament symbol twice instead of once, when the preceding note is a step lower or higher than the marked note. This is what the *port de voix* consists of. But it is not firmly determined whether this second note takes its value from the marked note or from the preceding note. In the manner in which M. d'Anglebert expresses it, it takes its value from the marked note, but I doubt that this is the best way to express the *port de voix* in harpsichord pieces. I know that this way is entirely appropriate for songs, but I find there to be few occasions where it is appropriate for pieces, and that the way that takes [the value of] the second note

---

1. As St Lambert implies, the failure of some harpsichord composers to include the *port de voix* in their ornament tables does not preclude its use in their compositions. Lebègue, for example, frequently writes out the *port de voix* in his two books of harpsichord pieces (1677 and 1687) although he makes no mention of it in his table.

2. This practice is often referred to today as 'over-legato' or 'legatissimo'. Nivers, in the preface of his *Premier livre d'orgue* (1665), also discusses this type of slur with specific reference to the *port de voix* (see Appendix B). This practice may be seen in the 18th century in Rameau's *Pièces de clavecin* of 1724, which gives virtually the same definitions of the slur as St Lambert and illustrates the *port de voix* as:

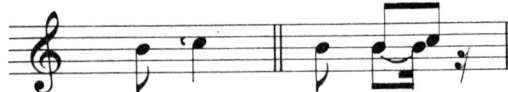

Cf. ch. VII for another use of the slur.

from the preceding one is much more suitable. Thus it is in the following manner that I would like to express the *ports de voix* given above.³

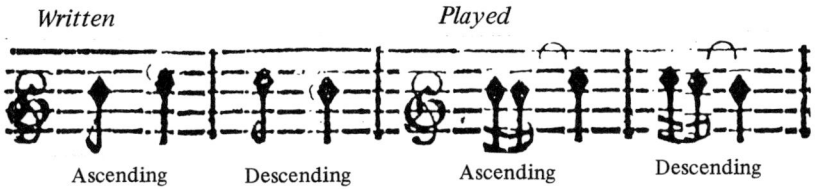

3. The difference of opinion between St Lambert and d'Anglebert over the rhythmic realization of the *port de voix* reinforces the evidence provided both by ornament tables and the music itself that there was no single 'correct' interpretation of this ornament in French music of the second half of the 17th century. Although there seems to have been a shift in taste from the time of Chambonnières to that of François Couperin, that is from a preference for *ports de voix* before the beat in the works of earlier composers to a preference for on-the-beat performance later, both on- and before-the-beat examples can be found throughout the period. Lebègue, who almost always writes out *ports de voix* as in the following example:

(*Premier livre de clavecin*, Sarabande grave in F major, mss. 7-8)

occasionally has an on-the-beat example.

(*Premier livre de clavecin*, Sarabande grave in G minor, ms. 3)

On the other hand, one can find numerous examples of written-out before-the-beat *ports de voix* in the works of d'Anglebert despite the unambiguous examples in his ornament table. See, for instance, the slurred notes in mss. 2-3 of the passacaille in appendix A. Even François Couperin's famous remark in *L'Art de toucher le clavecin* (Linde edn, p. 17) that the little note must strike with the harmony needs to be interpreted in light of the many places in his compositions where such a performance

Regarding the signs that can indicate the *port de voix*, the one M. d'Anglebert uses is good, but you should notice that it is notated like the one he uses for the *pincé* and that there is no difference between them, except that the sign for the *port de voix* is in front of the note it characterizes, and that of the *pincé* after.⁴ Sometimes he puts the two of them together, and in these places they mean a *port de voix* and a *pincé* together on the same note. This is what is called a *chute et pincé*, for he sometimes calls the *port de voix* a *chute*.⁵

results in unacceptable parallel intervals or other difficulties. The varying interpretations of the *port de voix* provide further proof, if any were needed, of the subtlety and expressivity of this ornament. St Lambert's statement that the manner of executing ornaments changes according to the pieces in which they are used (see p. 99) seems particularly applicable to the *port de voix*.

For an extremely thorough, if somewhat partisan, discussion of the evidence concerning various ways of performing the *port de voix* in France, see Frederick Neumann, *Ornamentation*, pp. 49-79.

4. The sign for the *port de voix* does not indicate whether the ornament should ascend or descend, however a corollary to St Lambert's 'rule of the *port de voix*' is that the musical context determines the direction of the ornament: if the preceding note is a step lower than the note bearing the *port de voix* sign, then the ornament ascends. If the preceding note is a step higher, the ornament descends.

5. A demonstration of the *chute et pincé* may be found in ch. XXIII, p. 84.

St Lambert does not discuss the fingering of the *port de voix*, but the examples of its use found in his two pieces at the end of the book show fingerings that Fr. Couperin called the 'old style' (*L'Art*, Linde edn, p. 16):

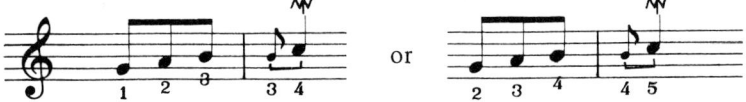

Couperin favored a change of fingers on the repeated note because it permitted more of a legato effect.

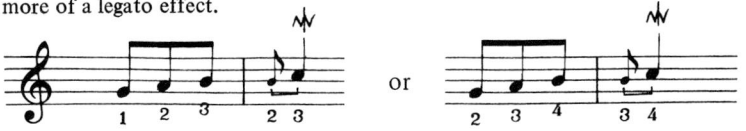

M. de Chambonnières acknowledges only the ascending *port de voix*, and he indicates it by a cross.⁶

6. Chambonnières's table actually has:

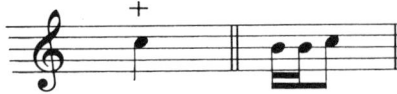

Despite what appears to be a clear musical example, Chambonnières's intentions regarding the performance of this ornament are not at all obvious. In his pieces, the ornament is always approached by step from below, as in the following example from the Sarabande in A minor (ms. 18) from his *Pièces de clavecin* of 1670:

Direct substitution of the realization from his table yields the following performance:

If this on-the-beat repetition of the ornamental note is the correct interpretation, it is unique to Chambonnières and in direct contrast to the practice of his contemporaries. A much more likely possibility is that the realization of the ornament in his table is inaccurately beamed and should actually be ♪♪ , or, in the context of the sarabande,

M. d'Anglebert does not explain how a *port de voix* is to be done when the preceding note is not on the neighboring degree to the marked note. However, in his pieces one finds *ports de voix* on notes whose preceding note is farther away.⁷ In order to complete what he omitted and to make all the necessary observations on this subject, we will say that it is necessary to distinguish three kinds of *ports de voix*: the *port de voix simple*, the *port de voix appuyé*, and the *demi port de voix*. All three may be done descending, but in ascending only the *port de voix simple* and the one called *appuyé* are used.

Concerning Descending *Ports de Voix*⁸

The *port de voix simple* is done by playing the note preceding the marked

This configuration is the one found in the works of Lebègue (see n. 3 above) and Nivers (see his table in appendix B and n. 10 below). St Lambert's presentation of Chambonnières's ornament, which includes the note before the ornament, is also rhythmically ambiguous owing to the missing eighth-note beat in the realization, but it does show that St Lambert considered the first sixteenth note in the realization to be not ornamental but what he calls the 'preceding note'. Given St Lambert's other musical examples in this chapter, he probably intended the two sixteenth notes to fall before the beat; at least the typesetter for the Roger edition of the *Principes* (c. 1710) assumed this to be the case when he corrected the example to read

7. Most of d'Anglebert's *ports de voix* are approached by step, usually from below. The others are most frequently approached by a third from above.

8. A number of musicians of the period, for example Étienne Loulié and Michel l'Affilard, use the term *coulé* or *coulement* to refer to the descending ornament and reserve the term *port de voix* for the ascending ornament.

one twice instead of once, assuming that this note is only one step higher than the marked note. As for the preceding note, it is never on the same pitch [as the note bearing the *port de voix*] and is always an eighth note or a quarter note.

The *port de voix appuyé* is done by playing the note that precedes and is only a step higher three times. This kind of *port de voix* is only appropriate to pieces that are played slowly and only when the preceding note is a quarter note, not an eighth.

When the preceding note is two steps higher than the marked note, it is no longer this note that is played twice to express the *port de voix*, but the one in between the preceding note and the marked note, that is, a borrowed note as for the *tremblement*. An example may be found below. In these instances, the *port de voix* is always *simple*: the one called *appuyé* would not be appropriate.

The *demi port de voix* is also only done on one occasion, and that is the one we just mentioned, when the preceding note is two steps higher. It consists of playing the borrowed note only once. See the example below. It is only suitable to pieces in quick duple time, such as rigaudons and airs which imitate their character.[9]

DESCENDING *PORTS DE VOIX*

Port de Voix simple.   Autre   Port de Voix appuyé. Demy Port de Voix.

9. The *demi port de voix*, a frequently used ornament, is usually called *tierce coulée* or *coulement*. Note that the sign for the *demi port de voix* is curved in the opposite direction from the other *port de voix* symbols. This particular symbol does not appear in d'Anglebert or the other harpsichordists.

MANNER OF PLAYING THEM

Port de Voix simple.   Autre   Port de Voix appuyé. Demy Port de Voix.

Concerning Ascending *Ports de Voix*

The *demi port de voix* is not done ascending, as I have already said, but only the other two, with the same observations as for the descending ones.

Written   Played

Port de Voix. simple. Port de Voix appuyé. Por de Voix simple. Port de Voix app.

The *port de voix appuyé* has more grace ascending than descending, but one must always remember that it is only beautiful in slow pieces and when the preceding note is a quarter note.[10]

I have never noticed any master putting a *port de voix* on a note whose preceding note is two steps lower; it would not have much grace in this instance. The *pincé* would be much more appropriate, and especially the one M. d'Anglebert calls *chute et pincé*, which is a composite of the *port de voix* and the *pincé*.

10. No other French theoretical source of the period discusses the ornaments St

Lambert calls the *autre port de voix simple* or the *port de voix appuyé*, although Nivers does illustrate the former in the preface to his *Livre d'orgue* of 1665 (see appendix B). Nonetheless, the *ports de voix* in these examples definitely reflect the ornamental practice of many of the French harpsichordists of the 1660s-80s, and even later, as may be seen in numerous passages from their works where such *ports de voix* are written out. The following passage is taken from Nivers, but similar passages may be found in the works of other composers, particularly in slow pieces such as sarabandes.

(Nivers, [*Premier*] *livre d'orgue*, Récit de voix humaine, mss. 14-16)

CHAPTER XXV

Concerning the Coulé

All the masters mention only one *coulé*, which is the one done on an ascending third. But M. d'Anglebert teaches six or seven types of *coulé*.[1] The first is the one done on a third that everyone uses. It consists of playing the lower of the two notes of the third before the higher, and while passing from the lower to the higher of also playing the one in between, releasing the middle note after having played it and only holding down the two notes of the third.

The finger that plays the note B must find itself in the air at the end of the *coulé*, and one must only hold down notes A and C for as long as the value of the notes of the third requires.[2]

1. Actually d'Anglebert shows only five types of *coulé*, but St Lambert includes as *coulés* two ornaments d'Anglebert calls *doubles chutes*. All but two of the *coulés* given in this chapter are taken directly from d'Anglebert's ornament table, using the same pitches and names. D'Anglebert's *coulés* are, however, more exact rhythmically.

2. St Lambert, Chambonnières, Lebègue, and d'Anglebert all show this ornament as starting on the beat.

All the masters indicate the *coulé* in the score by a little line drawn upwards between the two notes, as can be seen in the example above, but M. d'Anglebert indicates it by this other mark:

The same *coulé* can be done on a fourth in the same way by first playing the lower of the two notes and then the second, playing in passing the two that fill in the interval. These two must be released at the end of the *coulé*, because they are only borrowed notes, and one must only hold down the two that make up the fourth for as long as their value requires.[3]

The second *coulé* discussed by M. d'Anglebert is exactly like the first, since it is also done on a third, with the sole difference that it descends instead of ascending.[4]

3. This *coulé* is not given by d'Anglebert.
4. There should be an ascending quarter-note stem on the E in the realization of this ornament.

The mark placed after the third means that it is necessary to start the *coulé* from above. When it is in front, the *coulé* is started from below.

The third *coulé* is done on two consecutive notes, the second of which is two steps higher than the first. It is done as the *coulé* of the third is, except that after playing the first note, one repeats it in order to slur [*couler*] to the second by passing through the note in between, as in the *coulé* of a third.

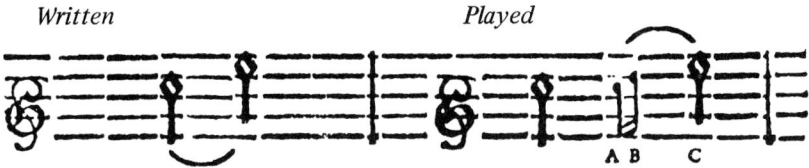

The fingers that played the borrowed notes A and B must find themselves in the air at the end of the *coulé*, and one should hold only the note C, for as long as its value requires.

The fourth *coulé* is also done on two consecutive notes, the second of which is three steps higher than the first. With that difference it is done just as the preceding one is, that is by repeating the first note after its value has expired in order to slur subtly to the second, passing through all the notes in between.

At the end of the *coulé*, all these borrowed notes are released and only the last note is held, for as long as its value requires.

The fifth *coulé* is also done between two consecutive notes at the same distance as the preceding example, but to express it one does not repeat the first note, as in the other. It is started on the second pitch.[5]

It is necessary, as in all the others, to release the borrowed notes at the end and to hold only the one that is essential, for as long as its value demands.

These last three types of *coulé* are only appropriate to slow pieces, and it is for this reason that these examples are given in half notes.

M. d'Anglebert, who is the inventor of these last three *coulés*, designates them all by the same sign, in which he seems to me to have made a mistake, for since these *coulés* are expressed differently, especially the second and the third, it is not a sufficient explanation to indicate them all in the same way. It is perplexing to a pupil who, seeing the sign between two notes, cannot distinguish which *coulé* he must do in that place, not yet being capable of judging which is the most appropriate there, and one must never leave any doubt in the minds of those one instructs. Therefore it would perhaps be more to the purpose to indicate every kind of *coulé*, except that of the third, by a little line drawn through the pitches of the notes to be borrowed for playing the *coulé*, in this manner:

This way of indicating *coulés* would remove the pupils' doubts, because they would know from the pitches occupied by the little line how many notes they have to borrow and where to borrow them.[6]

This little line would even be very suitable for expressing all kinds of *agréments* if its use were to be accepted. It would only be necessary to make it pass through all the pitches of the notes to be borrowed for doing

---

5. D'Anglebert also distinguishes these two *coulés* rhythmically. In the first, the value of the borrowed notes is taken from the first half note; in the other, they are played squarely on the second half note. See d'Anglebert's ornament table in appendix B, middle system, last two measures. In the absence of more examples it is difficult to know whether d'Anglebert indicated before-the-beat performance of the one *coulé* because it is done over four notes rather than three, as are the other, or whether he intended to suggest optional performance before the beat for *coulés* in general.

St Lambert's examples here do not provide any information regarding the rhythmic performance of this type of *coulé*, but see below, p. 93, where the example suggests performance before the beat.

6. Actually this idea appears to have already occurred to d'Anglebert. In his two examples of *coulés* between notes a fourth apart, the semicircular line indicating the ornament in the first departs clearly from the A, in the second from the B.

the *agrément*: for example, to indicate a *double cadence*, one would mark it thus:

But I have already said that one is free in the choice of ornaments and in the way of indicating them in the notation. This is why I only propose this simply without claiming that anyone is obliged to take my advice, reserving for myself alone the use of these signs in the pieces that I write for the persons I have the honor of teaching. This little line serves me well, especially for indicating certain *coulés* peculiar to me and which do not seem bad in the places where I use them, as for example in this:[7]

7. St Lambert's realization of this particular *coulé* shows it between the first and second beats of the measure, thus perhaps suggesting a preference on St Lambert's part for before-the-beat performance of *coulés* between consecutive notes. Cf. his stated preference for *ports de voix* before the beat, pp. 86-7.

The duration of the borrowed notes is regulated by the value of the marked note.[8]

The two other *coulés* taught by Mr. d'Anglebert are both done in the same way, except that one is done on a third and the other on a single note. He calls them *chutes*, marking and expressing them in this way:

It must always be remembered that one releases the borrowed notes at the end and holds only the essential ones, for as long as their value requires.

8. I.e. the speed of the ornament depends on the length of the note being ornamented: if it is long, the borrowed notes may be played slowly and still fit within the time of the note, but if it is short the ornament must be played more quickly. See also St Lambert's comment at the end of ch. XXVIII, 'Concerning the *Aspiration*', p. 98, that the speed of *coulés* and other ornaments depends on the tempo of the piece.

CHAPTER XXVI

Concerning the Arpégé

The *agrément* called *arpégé* or *arpègement* consists of separating the notes of a chord instead of playing them simultaneously, as was taught in the chapter concerning the voices [Chapter IX]. There are two kinds: the *arpégé simple*, which is done by simply separating the notes of the chord, and the *arpégé figuré*, in which notes other than those of the chord are borrowed in order to give it more charm.

The *arpégé simple* is done on chords of two, three, and four notes, but the *arpégé figuré* is only done on chords of three and four notes.[1]

MANNER OF INDICATING *ARPÉGÉS SIMPLES* IN THE NOTATION

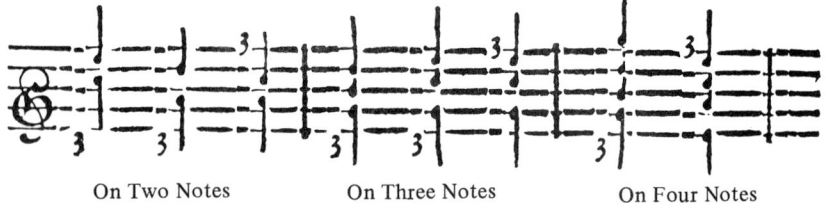

On Two Notes   On Three Notes   On Four Notes

MANNER OF PLAYING THEM

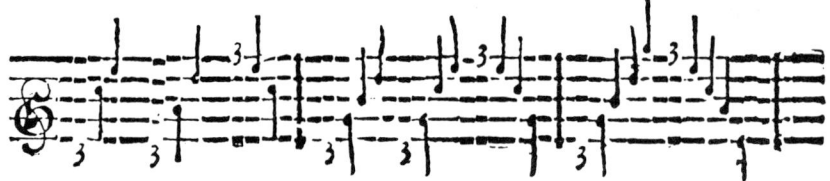

Arpéges start from either the bottom or the top, depending on whether the sign marking them is placed at the bottom or the top of the chord.[2]

In either the simple or figured *arpégé*, the fingers should apply themselves to the keys with such agility that no perceptible interval appears between the notes which could alter or break the rhythm of the piece.[3] The exception to this is the *arpégé* done on a two-note chord, for when there are several of these in a row, the notes have more grace by being noticeably separated, in such a way that the second note of each chord is reduced to half its value.

---

1. There are three errors in the musical examples in this chapter: (i) in the third chord of the first example, the pitches are not the same in the realization; (ii) in the second example, there is an incorrect B♯ in the sixth chord; (iii) in the fourth chord of the first example of *arpégés figurés* (p. 95), the semicircular symbol indicating the added note should be one step higher.

2. For appropriate fingerings for the *arpégé simple*, see the fingerings for broken chords, ch. XIX, p. 72.

3. This comment should be borne in mind when studying the very metrical examples of *arpégés* in d'Anglebert, Chambonnières, and Lebègue. See also St Lambert's statement at the end of the chapter on the *aspiration*, p. 99, that the speed of the *arpégé* and other ornaments depends on the tempo of the piece.

M. d'Anglebert does not notate his *arpéges* by the marks given in the above examples, but by a little line drawn on the diagonal through the stem of one of the notes of the chord:

This manner of notating *arpéges* should be preferred to all others, because it encumbers the score less.[4]

Concerning *Arpégés Figurés*

Arpégés figurés are played like the *arpéges simples* in the separation of the notes, but they also contain borrowed notes. There are some *arpéges* in which one borrows only one note, and others where one borrows two.

    4. Cf. St Lambert's comment in the Foreword, p. 7, where he states that he deliberately chose the symbol ₃ in his book because it is better known than any other.

MANNER OF INDICATING *ARPÉGÉS FIGURÉS*

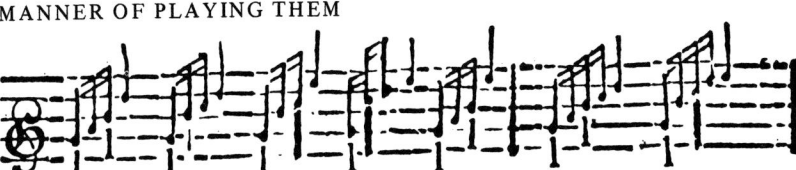

With One Borrowed Note   With Two Borrowed Notes

MANNER OF PLAYING THEM

At the end of the *arpége*, one must release all the borrowed notes and only hold down the essential ones, for as long as their value demands.[5]

The *arpége figuré* is almost always started from below, but when it must be started from above it has a little line slanting from upper left to lower right in the stem of the highest note.

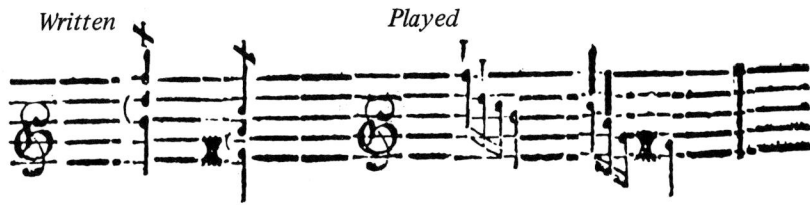

    5. D'Anglebert does not use the term *arpége figuré*, but calls a three-note chord with one borrowed note ***chute sur une note***, and with two borrowed notes ***chute sur deux notes***.

When the chord has four notes, there can be only one borrowed note in the *arpégé figuré*.

The position of the fingers which is most appropriate for *arpégés figurés* is the one taught in Chapter XIX for small hands.[6] The required borrowings do not allow the use of the fingerings indicated for large hands.[7]

6. See p. 71. In this case necessity overrides the principle of avoiding the use of the thumb in the right hand. The fingerings for small hands apply only to the *arpégés figurés* of three-note chords. There are obviously no options in the fingering of *arpégés figurés* of four-note chords.
7. Cf. St Lambert's comments about the use of *arpègement* in accompaniment in his *Nouveau traité de l'accompagnement*, p. 62.

CHAPTER XXVII

Concerning the Détaché

The last *agrément* of which M. d'Anglebert speaks is one that he calls the *détaché*. It is done before a *tremblement* or a *pincé* and consists of making a little silence between the *tremblement* or the *pincé* and the note preceding it, which is done by shortening the value of the preceding note a little.

The use of the *détaché* is very necessary in certain pieces with a lively tempo, particularly when the note preceding the *tremblement* is a step higher, and the note preceding the *pincé* a step lower than the note bearing the *agrément*. It is also not ungraceful in other pieces and on other occasions, but it is up to the good taste of the performer to judge the places where it should be done.

CHAPTER XXVIII

Concerning the Aspiration

To this last *agrément* I will add yet another that I call *aspiration*,[1] which consists of rapidly playing a single borrowed note only one time. It is indicated and expressed in this way.

MARK OF THE *ASPIRATION*   MANNER OF PLAYING IT

The mark indicating the *aspiration* is always placed after the note to be aspirated. When this mark has its point upwards, the upper neighbor note is borrowed, as for the *tremblement*. When it has the point downwards the lower note is borrowed, as for the *pincé*, which the above example demonstrates.[2]

---

1. This ornament, also known as the *accent*, does not appear in the ornament tables of the keyboard composers cited by St Lambert. Cf. Fr. Couperin, who uses the term *aspiration* to indicate not an added ornament but the shortening of a note.
2. Cf. St Lambert's use of a similar symbol for indicating the pitches borrowed for a *double cadence*, pp. 92-3.

These are the *agréments* in use among the best players of the harpsichord.

After having learned them here, the reader will be able to use them in all the occasions where he finds them to be appropriate, for as I have said so many times, the performer is extremely free in the choice of *agréments*. In the pieces he studies he may play them in places where they are not indicated, remove those that are there if he finds that they don't suit the piece, and add others to his liking. He may even, if he so desires, neglect all those that I have taught here (except the essential ones) and compose other new ones himself in accordance with his own taste, if he believes himself capable of inventing ones that are more beautiful. But he must be careful not to give himself too much freedom on this subject, especially in the beginning, for fear of spoiling what he wishes to embellish by trying to be too refined too soon. That is why it is good and even necessary to accept the *agréments* of others at first and to play them only in the places where they are indicated in the pieces until one is knowledgeable enough to judge without deceiving oneself that others wouldn't do any harm. The pupil must be persuaded, no matter how good his taste in regard to the harpsichord, that if he has only had six months of practice he cannot discern what gives playing grace as easily as those who have practiced the profession for twenty or thirty years and who through this long experience have acquired a more thorough knowledge of what can embellish their art. Thus, if he takes my advice, he will adhere to the *agréments* I teach in this book and that I propose with all the more liberty, since I have very little personal interest in their being followed, as there are very few of my own, all the rest coming from the most famous masters that our century has produced, which alone is sufficient to give them authority. But what is annoying about all this is that the reader will never thoroughly understand how all these *agréments* are to be executed, because it is impossible to explain them clearly in writing, since the manner of executing them changes according to the pieces in which they are used. And I can only say in general: *That the* agréments *must never alter the melody or the rhythm of the piece and that therefore in pieces of a lively tempo the* coulés *and* arpégés *must go by faster than when the tempo is slow; that one must never hurry in making an* agrément, *no matter how fast it must be played; that one must take his time, prepare his fingers, and execute it with boldness and freedom.*

But neither all this nor anything else I might say could render comprehensible a thing for which good taste is the only arbiter. It is extremely important, however, to know how to execute the *agréments* well, for without that knowledge they disfigure pieces instead of increasing their beauty, and it would be better not to do any at all than to do them badly. The resolution one should make from all this is to have a master who understands them well demonstrate them once or twice before one tries to put them into practice.

For all these *agréments* the number of notes to be borrowed in order to do them and the number of times they must be played are limited, except for the *tremblement*, which one plays as fast as possible, and the faster it is done, the more notes there are.

All the *agréments* in general follow the rule of the *tremblement* in regard to the notes to be borrowed for playing them, that is to say that one sometimes borrows accidentals, and sometimes naturals, according to the mode or the demands of the particular occasion. Reread the chapter on the *tremblement*; everything said there on this subject concerning the borrowed notes is applicable to all the other *agréments*.

Final Remarks

I have added two harpsichord pieces here at the end which put into practice all the principles of this method book. I have indicated the fingerings by numbers accompanying the notes, so that the reader may judge from the way I use the fingers in these places how he must use them in pieces he will wish to learn elsewhere. The principle to observe is to choose fingers which make the hand move the least, and to that end it is necessary when practicing to look ahead for several measures in a row in order to place the hand in the position necessary for playing them all with grace and facility.

Those who are not yet well versed in notation must realize that they will never learn a piece correctly without paying very close attention, because there will be several little things to observe that will undoubtedly escape them if they don't take very great care. When practicing one must observe:

1. What clefs are placed at the beginnings of the staves, in both the treble and the bass;
2. Whether the clefs change during the course of the piece, either at the beginning of a staff or in the middle;
3. Whether the clefs are accompanied by sharps or flats, which by transposing the piece make it necessary to play certain notes on the accidentals of the keyboard, not on the natural keys;
4. How many sharps or flats there are next to the clefs and what scale-degrees they are on;
5. Whether the clefs, after having been accompanied by accidentals, become simple again, or on the contrary whether, after having been simple, they become accompanied by accidentals;
6. What time signature is in effect at the beginning of the piece for determining its tempo;
7. Whether there is a new time signature in the course of the piece which changes the movement;
8. Which notes are to be played with the right hand and which with the left;
9. On what part of the harpsichord one must play these notes;
10. Whether there are several notes to be played simultaneously with a single hand;
11. That the notes above one another in a straight line from the bass to the treble are struck simultaneously;
12. Whether the two hands proceed together or whether they go separately. The notes of the treble proceed alone when there are no notes in the bass which correspond to them in a straight line, and likewise the notes of the bass proceed alone when there are none in the treble which correspond to them in a straight line;
13. Whether a note is marked with one of the three accidentals, sharp, flat, or natural;
14. Whether a note is marked by an *agrément*, such as a *tremblement*, a *double cadence*, a *pincé simple* or *appuyé*, a *port de voix simple*, *demi*, or *appuyé*, a *détaché*, etc.;

15. Whether a chord is marked with a *coulé* or an *arpégé*;

16. Whether when borrowing notes in order to do the *agréments* one plays a natural key when it is necessary to play an accidental, or on the contrary plays an accidental when it is necessary to play a natural;

17. Whether at the end of the *agréments* one releases the borrowed notes and only holds the essential ones, for as long as their value demands;

18. On what beat of the measure each note must be played and how long it must be held. Pupils err often in this regard;

19. Whether a note is followed by a dot that increases its value by half;

20. Whether a note is connected to another one by a tie or a slur;

21. Whether when there are several eighth notes in a row, one carefully observes the long and the short notes;

22. Whether one carefully observes rests in the voices and in the beats of the measure where they are indicated;

23. Whether one chooses good fingerings, in the right hand as well as the left;

24. Whether in the course of the piece there is a *renvoy* which indicates the repetition of some part of the piece;

25. Whether there is a difference between the endings of the repeated sections.

These observations are an abridged version of the entire method book, and one must have them continually before one's eyes.

MENUET.

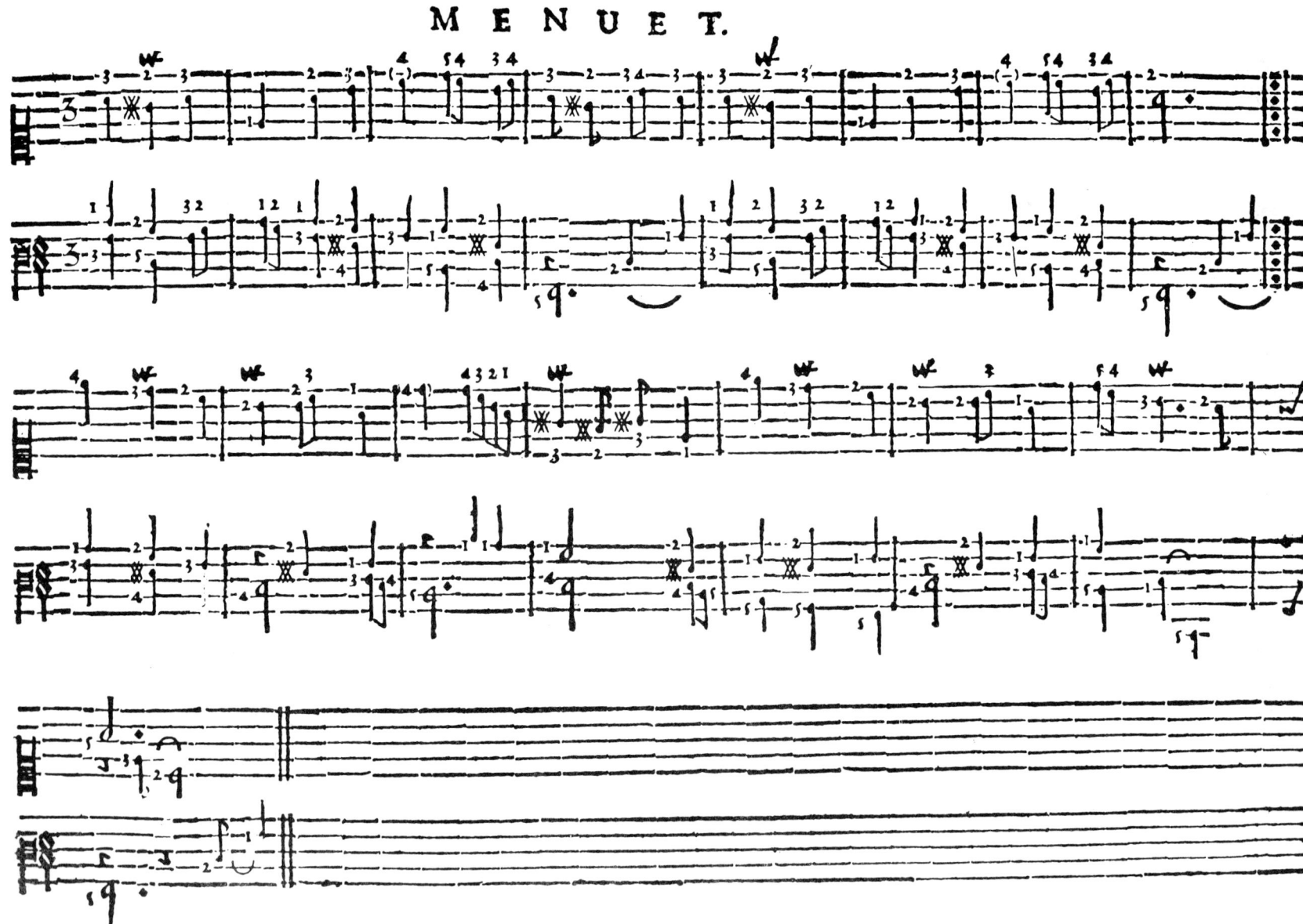

MENUET.

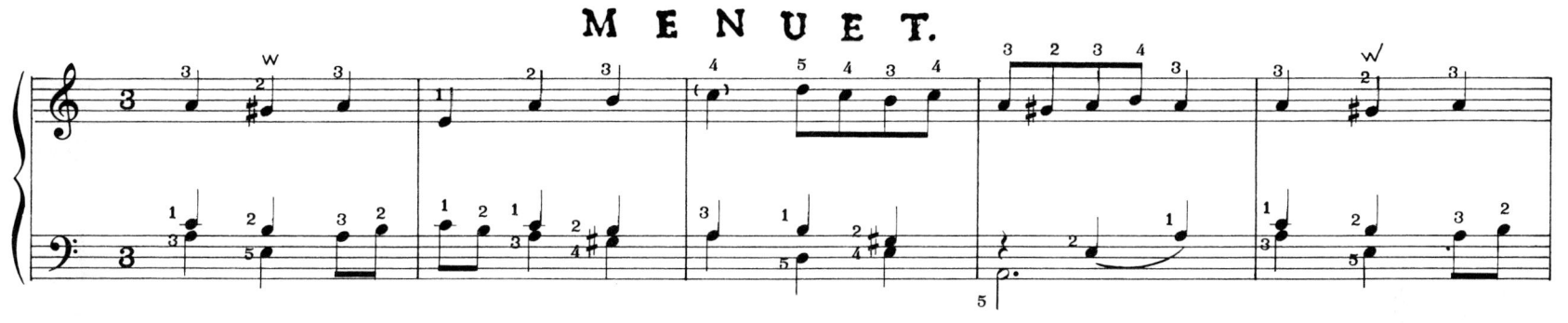
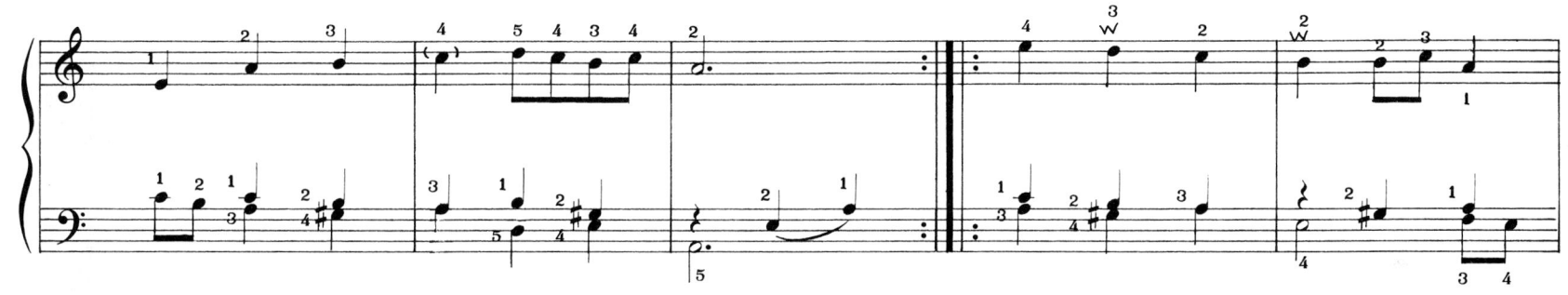

GAVOTTE.

GAVOTTE.

APPENDIX A

Pieces Cited by St Lambert

Nicolas Lebègue, *Pièces de clavecin* (Paris, 1677), p. 1.

From a copy in the Yale University Music Library.

Jean Henry d'Anglebert, *Pièces de clavecin* (Paris, 1689), p. 51

Jean Henry d'Anglebert, *Pièces de clavecin* (Paris, 1689), p. 29

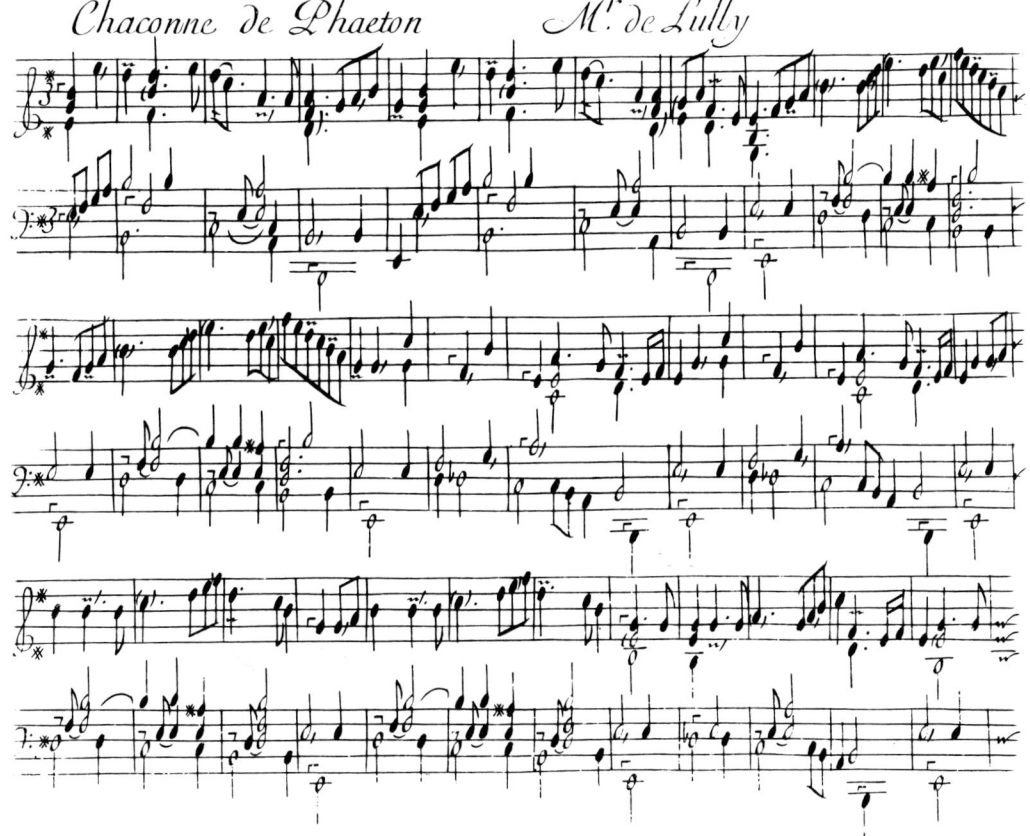

Jean Baptiste Lully, *Armide* (1686), reprise of the Overture. Ed. R. Eitner, Leipzig, 1885

Jean Baptiste Lully, *Armide* (1686), Act II, Sc. iv. Ed. R. Eitner, Leipzig, 1885

APPENDIX B

Ornament Tables of Composers Cited by St Lambert

Guillaume-Gabriel Nivers, [*Premier*] *Livre d'orgue* (Paris, 1665), preface: 'Observations Concerning Playing and Stops on the Organ[1]

Note that there are several things to observe regarding playing that are easier to demonstrate and comprehend at the keyboard than to express and understand on paper, since these things depend purely on execution and practice. Nevertheless, in order to give some instruction, [be sure to] pay attention to the correct position of the fingers, the clear equality of the *cadences* or *tremblements*, the different meter and tempo of pieces, and the articulation and subtle running together of the notes.

Concerning the Position of the Fingers

In order to play pleasingly, one must play easily; in order to play easily, one must play comfortably, and to this end one must arrange one's fingers gracefully on the keyboard, with suitability and equality, by curving the longer fingers a little in order to make them equal to the shorter ones, and by choosing the most suitable fingers for the different passages and chords. Here are examples of the most common and generally used [patterns]. 1 indicates the thumb or first finger, 2 indicates the second, and so on.

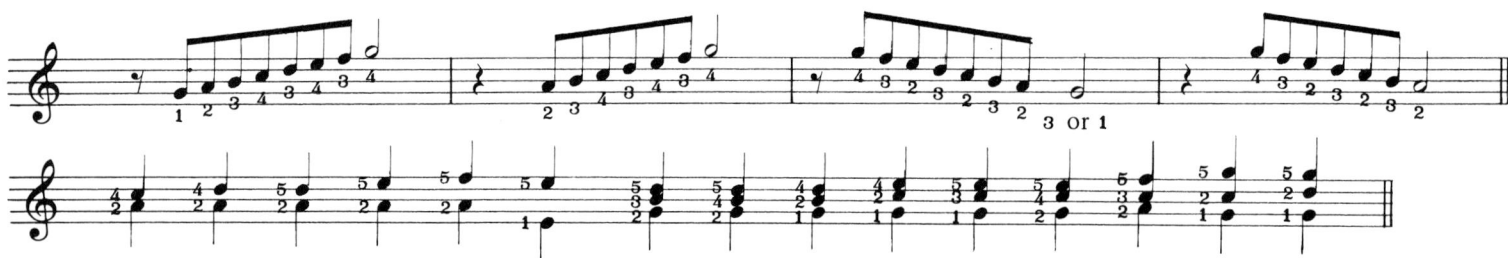

1. Only those portions of the preface directly relevant to St Lambert's book have been included in this translation, which is my own. The omitted sections are concerned with the eight church modes and with organ stops.

Concerning *Cadences* or *Tremblements*

Cadences or *tremblements* are played by alternately striking two neighboring keys equally and quickly. There are three kinds, named and indicated as follows: the *agrément* (∼), the *cadence* (ᴡ), and the *double cadence* (ᴡᴡ). Examples of them may be seen below, but first note that *tremblements* in general are played in four ways: (1) in the right hand with the third and fourth fingers; (2) also in the right hand with the second and third fingers; (3) in the left hand with the first and second fingers; and (4) also in the left hand with the second and third fingers. As to specifics, the *agrément* is usually played with the second and third fingers in the right hand, rarely with the third and fourth. In the left hand [it is played] with the first and second fingers, rarely with the second and third. The *cadence* is [sometimes] played with the second and third fingers in the right hand, but most often with third and fourth. In the left [it is sometimes played] with the second and third but most often with the first and second. The *double cadence* is always played with the third and fourth fingers in the right hand and is ended with the second finger in descending figures and with the fourth in ascending ones. In the left hand it is always played with the first and second fingers and is ended with the third finger in descending figures and with the first in ascending ones. Let us now come to a specific demonstration of these three types of *tremblement* where one may see the different ways of playing them according to their different contexts.

All the small notes are only for indicating the *tremblement*. The large note is the only one counted [in the measure] and since it is the main note one holds it a little after the striking [of the ornamental notes].

AGRÉMENT

CADENCE

DOUBLE CADENCE

Concerning the Meter and Tempo of Pieces
[*De la Mesure et du Mouvement des Pièces*]

Ordinarily there are considered to be three types of meter: that of the major time signature C in four beats, that of the minor time signature ¢ or binary time signature 2 in two beats, and that of the ternary time signature 3 in three beats. The two beats of the minor time signature or of the binary time signature are usually worth no more than two beats of the major time signature.[2] The three beats of the ternary time signature (or of the triple time signature) when there are several eighth notes in a measure are worth three beats of the major time signature, as on p. 101.[3] When there are only quarter notes or quarter and eighth notes interspersed in a measure, then these three beats are worth only half of the three beats of the major time signature, as on p. 28 near the middle.[4] But the three beats of the ternary time signature in *duos*, as on p. 60, are twice again as fast as the preceding and thus this meter is very rapid [*fort prompte*].[5]

The tempo of preludes, *fugues graves*, *basses et récits de voix humaine*, and *pleins jeux* is very slow [*fort lent*]; that of the other fugues, *diminutions*, *basses trompettes*, *récits de cromhorne*, *duos*, *cornets*, and *grands jeux* is livelier [*plus gay*]; and that of *duos* marked with the ternary time signature is very quick [*fort léger*]. There is another specific and very lively *mouvement* which is to place something like half dots after the first, third, fifth, and seventh eighth notes of each measure, assuming that there are eight of them; that is, to lengthen ever so slightly the above-mentioned eighth notes, and to shorten the others ever so slightly and proportionately. One may give this *mouvement* to the fugue on p. 14 and to other similar pieces. This [*mouvement*] is done at one's discretion, as are several other things that prudence and the ear must govern.

2. I.e. ♩ in ¢ or 2 is approximately twice as fast as ♩ in C.

3. I.e. ♩ in this type of 3 equals ♩ in C. Page references are to pieces in the 1665 print of Nivers's *Livre d'orgue*, from which this preface is taken. A modern edition of this book has been published by Éditions Bornemann.

4. In this piece the time signature 3 actually represents a $\frac{6}{4}$ meter, therefore ♩ in $\frac{6}{4}$ or in certain types of 3 equals ♩ in C.

5. Pieces such as this one are also actually in a $\frac{6}{4}$ meter with a ♩. ♪ ♩ ♩ ♪ ♩ rhythmic pattern. Nivers consistently marks them *légèrement*.

Concerning the Articulation and Running Together of the Notes
[*De la Distinction et du Coulement des Notes*]

It is a considerable ornament and elegance of playing to distinctly mark all the notes and to subtly slur [*couler*] some of them, which the manner of singing teaches properly. In order to articulate and mark the notes, it is necessary to lift the fingers early and not too high. For example, when playing a *roulade* or diminution on consecutive notes, you must promptly release one note while striking the next and so on for the others, for if you do not release the first until after striking the next, you will only blur rather than distinguish the notes.

In order to run the notes together, it is necessary to articulate them well, but you must not raise the fingers as promptly. This way is somewhere between articulation and confusion, or takes a little from each, and is practiced most frequently in *ports de voix* and in certain passages, examples of which follow. For all these things one must bear vocal practice in mind because in these instances the organ should imitate the voice.

Examples of the *Coulement* of the Notes

The two notes that must be run together the most are marked here by a little line.

Observe that there are certain thirds where there is a little line drawn between two notes in this way:

This means that you must play a very quick *coulade* on the third in this way:

and hold down the outside notes. Notice that the flat holds for all notes following it on the same degree. The same is true for the natural and the sharp.

PORTS DE VOIX

Jacques Champion de Chambonnières, *Pièces de clavessin* (Paris, 1670)

Nicolas Lebègue, *Les pièces de clavecin* (Paris, 1677)
From a copy in the Yale University Music Library.

Jean Henry d'Anglebert, *Pièces de clavecin* (Paris, 1689)

APPENDIX C

Compendium of St Lambert's Ornament Examples[1]

1. *Tremblements* **(pp. 76-82)**

---

1. In this transcription, obvious notational errors in the original, such as ornament symbols marked above the wrong note, have been corrected. All such errors are identified in the footnotes to the relevant chapters. St Lambert's rhythmic realization of the ornaments has been left as in the original. Page numbers refer to the location of the musical examples in the text.

Although St Lambert's purpose in a number of these examples is to reproduce the ornament tables of other composers, he does not always do so accurately, as a comparison with the originals in appendix B shows. Editorial comments regarding some of the more interesting discrepancies may be found in footnotes to the appropriate chapters.

Appendix C

Demonstration of the Symbols That Indicate the Different Kinds of *Tremblements* **According to M. d'Anglebert**

Tremblement simple | Tremblement appuyé | Cadence | Another [cadence] | Tremblement et pincé

Demonstration of the *Tremblements* According to M. Nivers

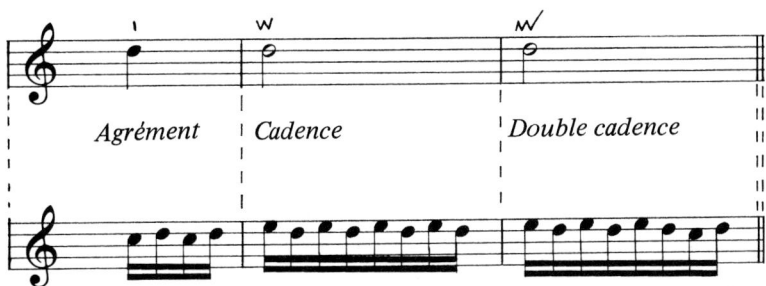

2. *Doubles Cadences* (pp. 83-4)

Appendix C

3. *Pincés* (pp. 84-5)

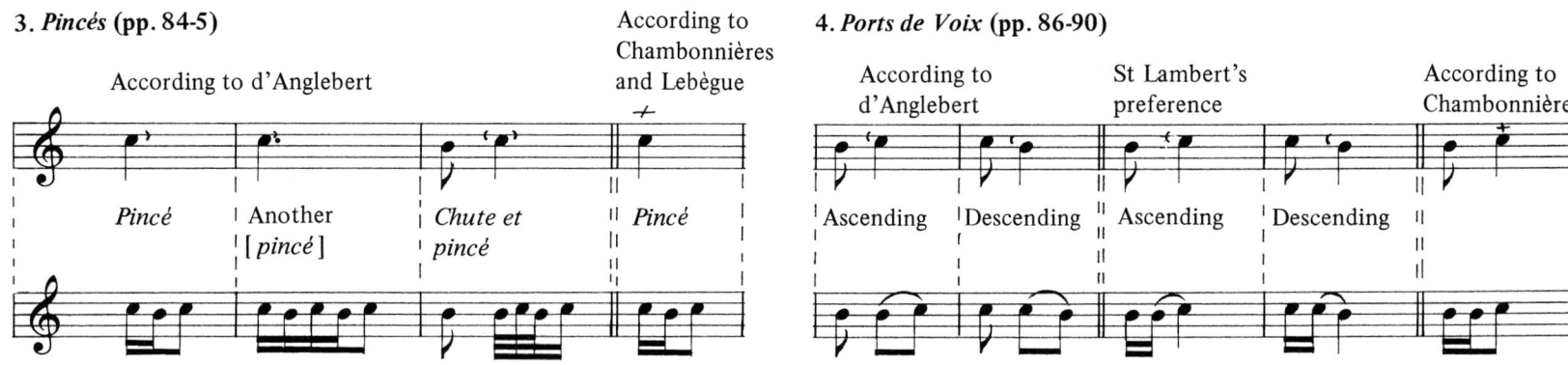

4. *Ports de Voix* (pp. 86-90)

5. *Coulés* (pp. 90-3)   D'Anglebert's symbol

St Lambert's Proposed Way of Notating Some *Coulés* and the *Double Cadence*

Appendix C

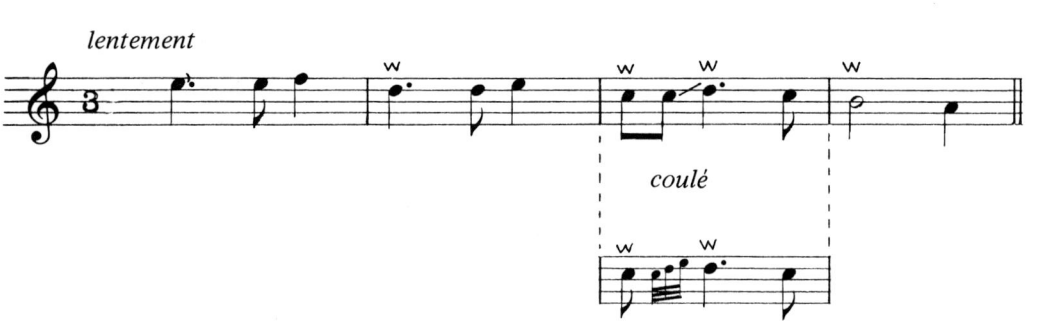

6. *Arpégé* or *Arpègement* (pp. 94-6)

Arpégés simples

Arpégés figurés

with one borrowed note

with two borrowed notes

7. *Détaché* (p. 97)

8. *Aspiration* (p. 98)

Fingering (pp. 71-4)

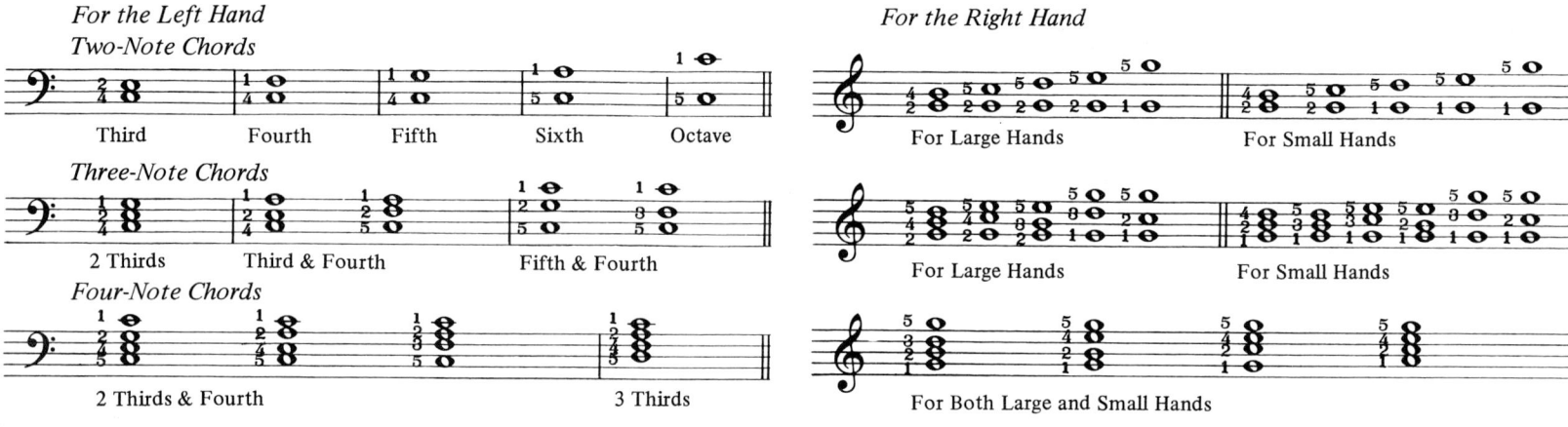

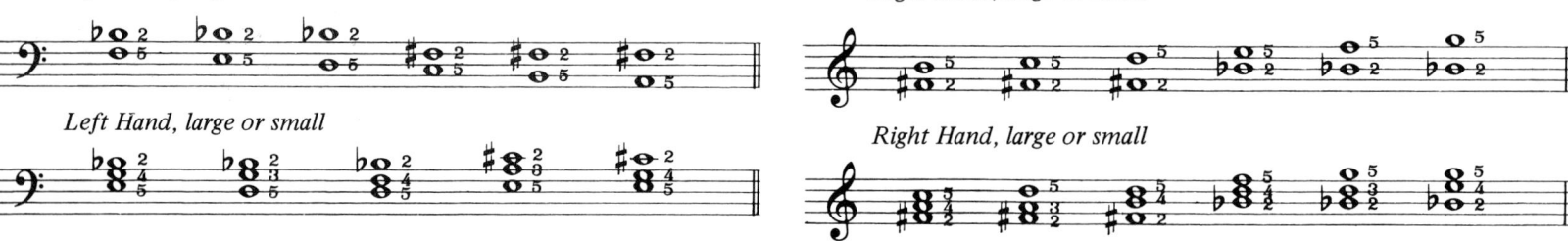

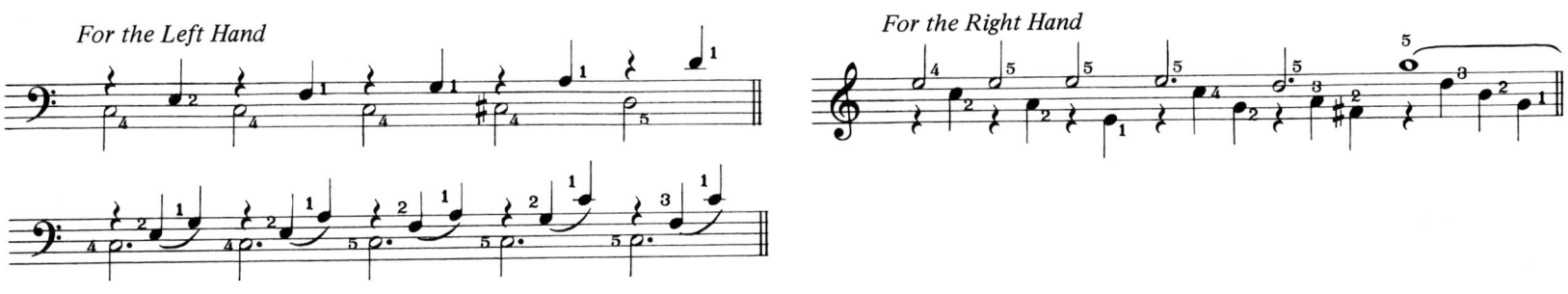

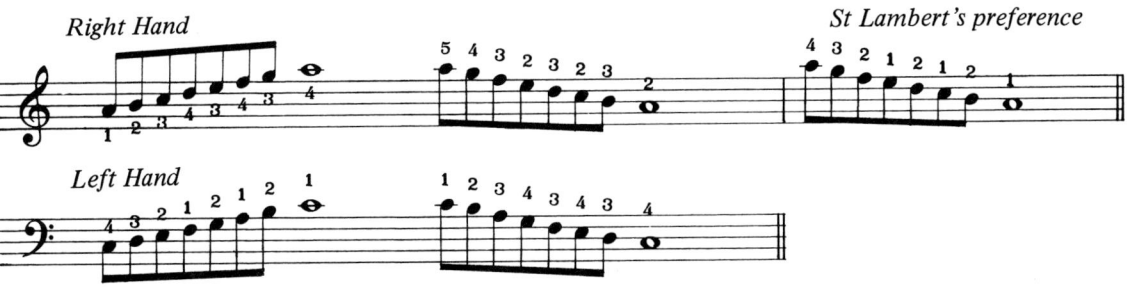

Bibliography

I. Seventeenth- and Eighteenth-Century Sources

Adlung, Jacob. *Anleitung zu der musikalischen Gelahrtheit.* Facsimile of the 1759 Erfurt edition. Kassel: Bärenreiter Verlag, 1953.

D'Anglebert, Jean Henry. *Pièces de clavecin.* Facsimile of the 1689 Paris edition. New York: Broude Brothers, 1965.

    Pièces de clavecin. Ed. Kenneth Gilbert. Paris: Heugel & Cie., 1975.

Boyer, Pascal. *Lettre à Monsieur Diderot, sur le projet de l'unité de clef dans la musique. Et la réforme des mesures, proposés par M. l'abbé La Cassagne, dans ses élémens du chant.* Amsterdam and Paris, 1767.

Brossard, Sébastien de. *Dictionaire de musique, contenant des termes Grecs, Latins, Italiens, et François les plus usitez dans la musique.* Facsimile of the 1703 Paris edition. Amsterdam: Antiqua, 1964.

Campra, André. *L'Europe galante.* Paris: J.B.C. Ballard, 1724; facsimile edition Farnborough: Gregg Press, 1967.

Chambonnières, Jacques Champion de. *Pièces de clavessin.* Facsimile of the 1670 Paris edition. Paris: Éditions Maurice Senart, 1925; reprinted New York: Broude Brothers, 1967.

    Œuvres complètes. Ed. Paul Brunold and André Tessier. New York: Broude Brothers, 1967.

Chaumont, Lambert. *Pièces d'orgue sur les huit tons* (Liège, 1696). Ed. Jean Ferrard. Paris: Heugel & Cie., 1970.

Clérambault, Louis Nicolas. *Pièces de clavecin* (Paris, 1704). Ed. Thurston Dart. Monaco: Éditions de l'Oiseau-lyre, 1964.

Couperin, François. *L'Art de toucher le clavecin.* Ed. Anna Linde. Leipzig: Breitkopf & Härtel Musikverlag, 1933.

    Pièces de clavecin, vols. I–IV. Ed. Kenneth Gilbert. Paris: Heugel & Cie., 1969.

Couperin, Louis. *Pièces de clavecin.* Ed. Alan Curtis. Paris: Heugel & Cie., 1970.

Dandrieu, Jean-François. *Trois livres de clavecin de jeunesse.* Ed. Brigitte François-Sappey. Paris: Heugel & Cie., 1975.

Démoz de la Salle. *Méthode de musique selon un nouveau système.* Paris, 1728.

Denis, Jean. *Traité de l'accord de l'espinette.* Facsimile of the 1650 Paris edition. Introduction by Alan Curtis. New York: Da Capo Press, 1969.

Dieupart, Charles [François]. *Six suites pour clavecin* (Amsterdam, 1702). Paris: Éditions de l'Oiseau-lyre, 1934.

Heinichen, Johann David. *Der Generalbass in der Komposition.* Facsimile of the 1728 Dresden edition. Hildesheim: Georg Olms Verlag, 1969.

Hotteterre, Jacques. *L'Art de préluder sur la flûte traversière, sur la flûte-à-bec, sur le haubois, et autres instrumens de dessus* (Paris, 1719). Ed. Michel Sanvoisin. Paris: A. Zurfluh, c. 1966.

Jullien, Gilles. *Premier livre d'orgue* (Paris, 1690). Ed. Norbert Dufourcq. Paris: Heugel & Cie., 1952.

[Laborde, Jean Benjamin de]. *Essai sur la musique ancienne et moderne.* 4 vols. Facsimile of the 1780 Paris edition. New York: AMS Press, 1978.

La Cassagne, Joseph. *Traité générale des élémens du chant.* Facsimile of the 1766 Paris edition. New York: Broude Brothers, 1967.

L'Affilard, Michel. *Principes très faciles pour bien apprendre la musique.* Facsimile of the 1705 Paris edition. Geneva: Minkoff Reprints, 1976.

La Guerre, Élisabeth Claude Jacquet de. *Pièces de clavecin* (Paris, 1707). Ed. Thurston Dart. Monaco: Éditions de l'Oiseau-lyre, 1965.

Lebègue, Nicolas. *Œuvres de clavecin* (1r. livre, Paris, 1677; 2e livre, Paris, 1687). Ed. Norbert Dufourcq. Monaco: Éditions de l'Oiseau-lyre, 1956.

Le Roux, Gaspard. *Pièces de clavecin* (Paris, 1705). Ed. Albert Fuller. New York: Alpeg Editions, 1959.

Loulié, Étienne. *Elements or Principles of Music* (Paris, 1696). Trans. Albert Cohen. New York: Institute of Mediaeval Music, 1965.

MS. Paris, Bibliothèque Nationale, fonds français, n.a. 6355, section XVI.

Lully, Jean Baptiste. *Armide.* Paris: Christophe Ballard, 1686.

Armide. Ed. T. de Lajarte. Chefs d'œuvre classiques de l'opéra français. Paris: T. Michaelis, n.d.

Armide, Acts I and II. Ed. Robert Eitner. Publikationen älterer praktischer und theoretischer Musikwerke, XIV Band, Dritter Theil. Leipzig: Brietkopf & Härtel, 1885.

Phaéton. Paris: Christophe Ballard, 1683.

Phaéton. Ed. T. de Lajarte. Chefs d'œuvres classiques de l'opéra français. Paris: T. Michaelis, n.d.

Marchand, Louis. *Pièces de clavecin* (Paris, 1702). Ed. Thurston Dart. Monaco: Éditions de l'Oiseau-lyre, 1960.

Masson, Charles. *Nouveau traité des règles pour la composition de la musique.* Facsimile of the second edition, Paris, 1699. Introduction by Imogene Horsley. New York: Da Capo Press, 1967.

Mattheson, Johann. *Grosse General-Bass-Schule.* Facsimile of the 1731 Hamburg edition. Hildesheim: Georg Olms Verlag, 1968.

Mémoires pour l'histoire des Sciences et des beaux Arts (*Journal de Trévoux*). Facsimile edition, Geneva: Slatkine Reprints, 1968. Issue dated juillet 1708.

Montéclair, Michel Pignolet de. *Principes de musique.* Paris, 1736.

Muffat, Georg. Foreword to *Florilegium Primum* (Augsburg, 1695). Ed. Heinrich Rietsch. Denkmäler der Tonkunst in Österreich, vol. II. Vienna: Artaria, 1894. English translation in Oliver Strunk, *Source Readings in Music History* (New York: W.W. Norton & Co., 1950), 442-5.

Nivers, Guillaume-Gabriel. [*Premier*] *livre d'orgue* (Paris, 1665). Ed. Norbert Dufourcq. Paris: Éditions Bornemann, 1963.

Second livre d'orgue (Paris, 1667). Ed. Norbert Dufourcq. Paris: Éditions de la Schola Cantorum, 1956.

Quantz, Johann Joachim. *On Playing the Flute.* Trans. Edward R. Reilly. New York: Schirmer Books, 1966.

Raison, André. *Premier livre d'orgue* (Paris, 1688). Ed. Norbert Dufourcq. Paris: Éditions de la Schola Cantorum, 1963.

Second livre d'orgue (Paris, 1714). Ed. J. Bonfils. Paris: Éditions de la Schola Cantorum, n.d.

Rameau, Jean-Philippe. *Pièces de clavessin.* Facsimile of the 1724 Paris edition. New York: Broude Brothers, 1967.

Pièces de clavecin. Collected works 1706-1747, with the composer's original appended text unabridged. Ed. Erwin R. Jacobi. Kassel: Bärenreiter Ausgabe, 1958.

Traité de l'harmonie. Facsimile of the 1722 Paris edition. New York: Broude Brothers, 1965.

Treatise on Harmony. Trans. Philip Gossett. New York: Dover Publications, 1971.

Rousseau, Jean. *Méthode claire, certaine et facile pour apprendre à chanter la musique.* 4th edition. Amsterdam: Estienne Roger, [1691].

Rousseau, Jean-Jacques. *Dictionnaire de musique.* Facsimile of the 1768 Paris edition. Hildesheim: Georg Olms Verlag, and New York: Johnson Reprint Corp., 1969.

Saint Lambert, Monsieur de. *Nouveau traité de l'accompagnement du clavecin, de l'orgue, et des autres instruments.* Paris: Christophe Ballard, 1707; facsimile edition Geneva: Minkoff Reprints, n.d.

Les Principes du clavecin. Paris: Christophe Ballard, 1702; facsimile edition Geneva: Minkoff Reprints, n.d.

Walther, Johann Gottfried. *Musikalisches Lexikon.* Facsimile of the 1732 Leipzig edition. Kassel: Bärenreiter Ausgabe, 1953.

II. Nineteenth- and Twentieth-Century Sources

Aldrich, Putnam C. 'The principal *agréments* of the seventeenth and eighteenth centuries: a study in musical ornamentation'. Ph.D. dissertation, Harvard University, 1942.

Anthony, James R. *French Baroque Music from Beaujoyeulx to Rameau.* Revised edition, New York: W.W. Norton & Co., 1978.

Arnold, F.T. *The Art of Accompaniment from a Thorough-Bass.* London: Oxford University Press, 1957.

Barbour, J. Murray. *Tuning and Temperament: A Historical Survey.* East Lansing: Michigan State College Press, 1953.

Bénoit, Marcelle. *Musiques de cour: chapelle, chambre, écurie, 1661-1733.* Paris: Éditions A. & J. Picard, 1971.

Versailles et les musiciens du roi, 1661-1733. Paris: Éditions A. & J. Picard, 1971.

Borrel, Eugène. 'Les Indications métronomiques laissées par les auteurs français du 18e siècle', *Revue de Musicologie* (1928), 149-53.

L'Interprétation de la musique française (de Lully à la Révolution). Paris: Librairie Félix Alcan, 1934.

Brenet, Michel. 'La Librairie musicale en France de 1653 à 1790, d'après les registres de privilèges', *Sammelbände der Internationalen Musikgesellschaft* (1906-7), 401-66.

Bukofzer, Manfred F. *Music in the Baroque Era.* New York: W.W. Norton & Co., 1947.

Burchill, James F. 'Saint Lambert's *Nouveau traité de l'accompagnement*: a translation and commentary'. Ph.D. dissertation, University of Rochester, 1979.

Camesi, David. 'Eighteenth-century conducting practices', *Journal of Research in Music Education* 18 (1970), 365-76.

Camus, Raoul. 'On the cadence of the march', *Journal of Band Research* 16:2 (Spring 1981), 13-23.

Carse, Adam. *The Orchestra in the XVIIIth Century.* Cambridge: W. Heffer & Sons, Ltd., 1940.

Dart, Thurston. 'On Couperin's harpsichord music', *Musical Times*, vol. 110, no. 1516 (June 1969), 590-4.

Devriès, Anik. *Édition et commerce de la musique gravée à Paris dans la première moitié du 18e siècle.* Geneva: Éditions Minkoff, 1976.

Donington, Robert. *The Interpretation of Early Music.* New version, London: Faber & Faber, 1974.

Doursther, Horace. *Dictionnaire universel des poids et mesures anciens et modernes.* Facsimile of the 1840 Brussels edition. Amsterdam: Meridian Publishing Co., 1965.

Eppelsheim, Jürgen. *Das Orchester in den Werken Jean-Baptiste Lullys.* Tutzing: Hans Schneider Verlag, 1961.

Fajon, Robert. 'Propositions pour une analyse rationalisée du récitatif de l'opéra lullyste', *Revue de Musicologie* 64 (1978), 55-75.

Fétis, F.-J. *Biographie universelle des musiciens et bibliographie générale de la musique.* Paris: Librairie de Firmin-Didot, 1878.

Forkel, Johann Nicolaus. *Allgemeine Literatur der Musik.* Facsimile of the 1792 Leipzig edition. Hildesheim: Georg Olms Verlag, 1962.

Fuller, David. 'Eighteenth-century French harpsichord music'. Ph.D. dissertation, Harvard University, 1965.

'French harpsichord playing in the seventeenth century - after Le Gallois', *Early Music* 4 (1976), 22-6.

Review of James R. Anthony, *French Baroque Music*, in *Journal of the American Musicological Society* 28 (1975), 374-84.

Gaspari, Gaetano. *Catalogo della Biblioteca del Liceo Musicale di Bologna*, vol. I: *Opere Teoriche*. Bologna: Libreria Romagnoli dall'Acqua, 1890.

Gerber, Ernst Ludwig. *Historisch-Biographisches Lexikon der Tonkünstler.* Facsimile of the 1790-92 Leipzig edition. Graz: Akademische Druck- u. Verlagsanstalt, 1977.

Neues Historisch-Biographisches Lexikon der Tonkünstler. Facsimile of the 1812-14 Leipzig edition. Graz: Akademische Druck- u. Verlagsanstalt, 1966.

Gustafson, Bruce. 'A letter from Mr Lebègue concerning his preludes', *Recherches sur la musique française classique* 17 (1977), 7-14.

Harris-Warrick, Rebecca. 'The tempo of French baroque dances: evidence from 18th-century metronome devices', *Proceedings of the 1982 Meeting of the Dance History Scholars.* Cambridge, Mass., 1982.

Houle, George. 'The musical measure as discussed by theorists from 1650 to 1800'. Ph.D. dissertation, Stanford University, 1960.

Hubbard, Frank. *Three Centuries of Harpsichord Making.* Cambridge, Mass.: Harvard University Press, 1965.

Kirkpatrick, Ralph. 'Eighteenth-century metronomic indications', *Papers of the American Musicological Society* (1938), 30-50.

'On re-reading Couperin's *l'Art de toucher le clavecin*', *Early Music* 4 (1976), 3-11.

Lesure, François. *Bibliographie des éditions musicales publiées par Estienne Roger et Michel-Charles Le Cène (Amsterdam 1696-1743).* Paris: Société Française de Musicologie and Heugel & Cie., 1969.

Lindley, Mark. 'Instructions for the clavier diversely tempered', *Early Music* 5 (1977), 18-23.

Neumann, Frederick. *Ornamentation in Baroque and Post-Baroque Music, with Special Emphasis on J.S. Bach.* Princeton: Princeton University Press, 1978.

Powell, Newman Wilson. 'Early keyboard fingering and its effect on articulation'. Master's thesis, Stanford University, 1954.

Russell, Raymond. *The Harpsichord and Clavichord.* New York: W.W. Norton & Co., 1973.

Schilling, Gustav. *Encyclopädie der gesammten musikalischen Wissenschaften, oder Universel-Lexikon der Tonkunst.* Stuttgart: Verlag von Franz Heinrich Kohler, 1840.

Wolf, R. Peter. 'Metrical relationships in French recitative of the 17th and 18th centuries', *Recherches sur la musique française classique* 18 (1978), 29-49.

Zaslaw, Neal. 'Materials for the life and works of Jean-Marie Leclair l'aîne'. Ph.D. dissertation, Columbia University, 1970.
    'Mozart's Tempo Conventions', *Report of the Eleventh Congress of the International Musicological Society* (Copenhagen, 1972), 720-33.
Zenatti, Arlette. 'Le Prélude dans la musique profane de clavier en France, au 18e siècle', *Recherches sur la musique française classique* 5 (1965), 169-84.
Zupko, Ronald Edward. *French Weights and Measures before the Revolution.* Bloomington: Indiana University Press, 1978.

Index

Numbers followed by the letter n refer to the Editor's footnotes, those by the letter R to St Lambert's 'Remarks'. Numbers in italics refer to material in the appendices.

accent, 97n
accidentals, 19, 60-9, 100-1, *115*
    cancellation of, 64n
    effect on fingering of, 71-2, 73n
    in *tremblements*, x, 78-80, 99, *113-14*
    on keyboard, 18-19
Adlung, Jacob, x
agrément of Nivers, 82, 84, *113*, *121*
agréments, xii, 75-99, 100-1, *113-25*; see also under individual names
    choice of, 98-9
    notational reforms in, 92-3
    speed of, 93, 99
    tables of, *113-17*, *118-25*
airs d'opéra
    changes in meter in, 46
    on harpsichord, 44-5, 57, *109*
allemandes, 39n, 46, 47
d'Anglebert, Jean Henry, vii, ix, xii-xiii, 7n, 14n, 29n, 38n, 43R, 56n, 57n, 59n, 78n, 81-2, 83n, 84, 85n, 86-9, 90-3, 94n, 95, 97, *108-9*, *117*, *120*, *122-4*
aptitude for harpsichord, 5
Armide (Lully)
    air from, 45, *111*
    overture to, 45, *110*
    passacaille from, 57

arpégé, 7, 75, 94-6, 99, 101, *116*, *117*, *124-5*
    fingerings for, 94n, 96
    speed of, 99
arpègement, 94, 96n, *116*, *124*; see also *arpégé*
l'Art de toucher le clavecin (Fr. Couperin), xi, xii, 73n, 74n, 76n, 77n, 87n
aspiration, 98, *125*

Bach, Johann Sebastian, xiii
Ballard, Christophe, viii, x, 1, 24n
beating time, 33, 35-43, 47
    audible, 39
    difficulties in, 39-42
    mechanics of, 38-9
bourées, xviii, 39n, 47
Boyer, Pascal, xiv-xvi, xvii n
Brossard, Sébastien de, x

cadence, 81-2, 83, *112-14*, *116*, *117*, *120*, *121*; see also *tremblement*
    double: see double cadence
Campra, André, ix, 43R
canaries, xviii n, 35n, 39n
Chaconne from *Phaéton* (Lully/d'Anglebert), 57, *109*
chaconnes, xvii, 39n, 56-7
Chambonnières, Jacques Champion de, vii, ix, xii-xiii, 7n, 14n, 25n, 78n, 82, 84, 85, 87n, 88, 90n, 94n, *116*, *122*
chanson, repetitions in, 56-7
Chaumont, Lambert, 78n
children, teaching of, xi, 5, 6, 15R

chords
    broken, 72-3, 94-6, *124-5*
    definition of, 70
    fingering of, 71-3, *112-13*, *126-7*
chronometer, 24n, 44n
chute, 87, 93, *117*, *124*; see also *port de voix*
    chute et pincé, 84-5, 87, 89, 102-5, *117*, *122*
    double, 90, *117*
    sur une note, 95n, *117*
    sur deux notes, 95n, *117*
clefs, 9-22, 100
    and key signatures, 68-9
    correspondence to keyboard of, 19, 21-2
    explanation of, 9-14
    method for learning, 14-17
    reform of, x, xiv, 14-16R
    use in harpsichord music, 14, 102, 104, *107-9*
    use in situating pitches, 21-2
coulade, *115*; see also *coulé*
coulé, 75, 88n, 90-3, 99, 101, *115*, *116*, *117*, *123-4*
coulement, 88n, 89n
Couperin, François, vii, xi, xii, xiii, 16n, 73n, 74n, 76n, 77n, 78n, 87n, 98n
Couperin, Louis, vii, ix, 29n
couplets, 56-7, 59, *108-9*
courantes, 39n, 45, 47

Dandrieu, Jean-François, 73n
Démoz de la Salle, xvii
Denis, Jean, 63n, 74n
détaché, 97, 100, *117*, *125*

135

Dieupart, Charles [François], 78n
diminutions, 74, 77R, *112-13*, *115*
direct, 59, 102, 104
Diruta, Girolamo, vii n
dot, 26, 101
double bar, 56-7, 102-5
double cadence, 82, 83-4, 93, 100, *113-14*, *116*, *117*, *121*, *123*

l'Europe galante (Campra), 43R

fingering, x, 70-4, 100-1, *112-13*, *126-7*
   of *arpégés*, 94n, 96
   of chords, 71-3, *112-13*, *126-7*
   of diminutions, 74, 77R, *112-13*, *127*
   of pieces by St Lambert, 102-5
   of *ports de voix*, 87n
   of tremblements, 76-7R, *113*
fingers
   action of, 74, *115*
   agility of, 76-7R, 94
   height of, 74, *115*
   incorrect use of, 7
   position of, 70-4, *112-13*
flat, xiii, 19, 60, 62-3, 64, 65-6R, 67-9, 100, *115*
   as cancelling a sharp, 63, 64n
   cancellation of, 63, 64n, 69
   effect on fingering of, 71-2, 73n
   in key signatures, 67-9
   in *tremblements*, x, 78-80
   keys on keyboard, 18-19

gaillardes, 39n
gamut, 10R
Gavotte by St Lambert, 58, 59, 104-5
gavottes, xviii, 39n
gigues, 35n, 39, 42-3R, 45n, 47
guidon: see direct

hand
   aptitude of, 5
   placement of, 7
   position of, 74
harpsichord
   aptitude for, 5
   double manual, 20
   keyboard of, 8, 18-20
   method books for, vii, 3-4
   qualities of, 3, 48
   range of, 19-20
harpsichord pieces
   arrangements of opera airs, 44-5, 57, *109*
   as teaching tools, 6
   choice of *agréments* in, 98-9
   examples of, 49-50, 53-4, 56-7, 102-5, *107-9*
   repetitions within, 56-7, 58, 59, 100
   rhythm of *port de voix* in, 86-7
   structure of, 56-7
   texture of, 49-50
   use of clefs in, 14
harpsichord teachers (masters)
   failings of, 6-7
   qualities of, 6-7
   re fingering of *tremblement*, 76-7R
   St Lambert as, vii, ix, xi, xiv, 3-4, 14-16R
   use of ornaments of, 97-8
Heinichen, Johann David, x
hexachords, 10n, 15n
Hotteterre, Jacques, xvi-xviii

inequality, rhythmic, 25R, 46, 101, *114*

Journal de Trévoux, x-xi
Jullien, Gilles, 84n

keyboard, 1, 8, 18-20
   accidentals on, 19, 61, 62-3, 64-6, 73n
   double manual, 20
   illustration of, 18
   names of keys on, 18-20, 21-2, 64-6R
   range of, xi, 19-20
   short octave, 19-20
key signatures, 66, 67-9, 79-80, 100
   reform of, xiii

Laborde, Jean Benjamin de, xiv n
La Cassagne, Joseph (Abbé), xiv, 16n
L'Affilard, Michel, 88n
Lambert, Michel, as confused with St Lambert, ix
league, length of, xv
Lebègue, Nicolas, vii, ix, xii-xiii, 7n, 29n, 56n, 78n,
   82, 84n, 85, 87n, 88n, 90n, 94n, *107*, *116*, *122*
Leclair, Jean-Marie l'aîné, xviii
Le Roux, Gaspard, xiii, 78n
Loulié, Étienne, x, xvi-xvii, 10n, 24n, 44n, 88n
loures, 35n, 39n
Lully, Jean Baptiste, ix, xiii, xviii, 39n, 45, 46, 48n,
   57n, *109*, *110-11*

Masson, Charles, xvi, xvii
Mattheson, Johann, x
measures, 32-43, 46-7
   definition of, 32
   incomplete, 46-7, 104-5
   number of beats in, 33-9, 43
   value of rests in, 52-5
Menuet by St Lambert, 56n, 102-3
menuets, xvii, 38, 39n
   tempo of, 38
Mersenne, Marin, vii n
meter, xi, xiv-xix, 32-47, *114*; see also time signatures
   change of, 46
   types of, 42-3
method books for harpsichord, vii, 3-4
Montéclair, Michel Pignolet de, xiv, xvi-xvii, xviii n,
   16n
Muffat, Georg, xviii

natural, 60, 64-6, 79-80, 100-1, *115*
Nivers, Guillaume-Gabriel, xii-xiii, xviii, 73n, 74n, 76n, 78n, 82, 84, 86n, 88n, 90n, *112-15*, *121*
notation, xi, 1, 8, 9R, 100-1; see also under specific notational symbols, e.g. clefs
    reform of, xiii-xiv, 14-16R, 45, 92-3, 123
notes, 8, 9-17, 100-1
    beaming of, 24-5
    double stemming of, 50, 104-5
    location on keyboard of, 21-2, 100
    names of, 9-17
    with accidentals, 60-9, 100
notes inégales: see inequality, rhythmic
note values, 23-5, 26, 27-8, 29-31, 101
    compound, 26, 27-8, 40-1
    dotted, 26, 101
    syncopated, 41-2
    tied, 27-8, 40-1, 101
    unequal, 25R, 46, 101, *114*
Nouveau traité de l'accompagnement (St Lambert), viii, x, xiii, 67n, 96n

Opéra (Académie Royale de Musique), 44-5
ornaments: see *agréments*, and see under individual names
Overture to *Armide* (Lully), 45, *110*
overtures, xviii, 35n, 38n, 46

Passacaille from *Armide* (Lully/d'Anglebert), 57
Passacaille in G minor (d'Anglebert), 56n, 59n, *108*
passacailles, xvii, 39n, 56-7
passepieds, xviii n, 39
pavannes, 45n
petite reprise, 58n, 104-5, *116*
Phaéton (Lully), 46, 57, *109*
pièces de clavecin: see harpsichord pieces
pincé, 7, 75, 82, 84-5, 87, 89, 97, 98, 100, 102-5, *116*, *117*, *122*
    tremblement et pincé, 81-2, *117*

chute et pincé, 84, 87, 89, 102-5, *117*, *122*
pincement, 84n, 85n, *116*; see also *pincé*
port de voix, xii, 75n, 86-90, 100, *108*, *115*, *116*, *117*, *122*; see also *chute*
    and use of slur, 86, *108*, *115*
    fingering of, 87n
    rhythm of, xii, 86-8, *122*
preludes, xi, xviii, 29n, 31R, *107*
Principes du clavecin (St Lambert)
    contents of, xi-xii
    context of, xii-xiii
    importance of, vii
    influence of, x-xi
    publication of, viii-ix
    Roger edition of, viii, x, 88n

quarter notes
    inequality of, 46
    in various meters, 36-8, 49-50
    speed of, xv-xvi, 24, 35-6, 43n, 44

Raguenet, François, 39n
Raison, André, 25n, 73n, 78n
Rameau, Jean-Philippe, x, 16n, 30n, 73n, 74n, 86n
recitative, xvii-xviii, 46
reform
    of clef notation, x, xiv, 14-16R
    of key signatures, xiii
    of notation of some *agréments*, 92-3, *123*
    of time signatures, xiii-xiv, 45
'Remarks', xix, 1, 9, 9-10, 14-16, 19, 25, 26, 27, 31, 42-3, 64-6, 67, 70, 76-7, 100-1
renvoy, 58, 59, 101, 104-5, *108*, *116*
repetition, ways of indicating, 56-7, 58, 59, 102-5, *108*
reprise, 32, 45, 56, *110*
    petite: see *petite reprise*
rests, 51-5, 101, 102-5, *107-9*
rhetoric, compared to music, 32-3

rhythmic inequality; see inequality, rhythmic
rigaudons, 39n, 47, 89
Roger, Estienne, viii, x, 88n
Rousseau, Jean, xvii
Rousseau, Jean-Jacques, xvi

Saint Lambert
    as composer, viii
    as poet, viii
    as teacher, vii, ix, xi, xiv, 3-4, 14-16R
    as theorist, vii, xii, xiii-xix
    influence of, x-xi
    information about, ix
    on meter and tempo, xiv-xix
Santa María, Tomás de, vii n
sarabandes, xvii, 39n, 88n
semitone, 64-6R
sharp, 19, 60, 61-2, 63, 64-6R, 67-9, 100, *115*
    as cancelled by flat, 63, 64n
    as substitute for natural, 64
    cancellation of, 61-2, 64n, 69
    effect on fingering of, 71-2, 73n
    in key signatures, 67-9
    in *tremblements*, x, 78-80
    keys on keyboard, 18-19
short octave, 19-20
slur, x, xi, 29-31, 101, 102-5, *115*
    and fingering, 72-3
    distinguished from tie, x, 29-30
    use in *port de voix* of, 86, *108*, *115*
    use in preludes of, xi, 29n, 31R, *107*
spinet, 20; see also harpsichord
staff, x, 9-10, 49, 59
    different types of, 9R
    directs on, 59
syncopation, 41-2
system of Si, 10n, 15-16R

teachers, harpsichord: see harpsichord teachers

temperaments, 19n, 62n, 67n
tempo, xi, xiv-xix, 24, 32-47, 100, *114*
    as based on quarter note, xv-xvi, 24, 35-6, 37, 38
    as related to time signatures, xiv-xix, 35-9, 42-5, *114*
    chart of, 43n
    difficulty of indicating, 43-5
    of menuet, 38
    verbal indications of, xvii, 44-5, *111*, *124*
tie, x, 27-8, 101, 104-5
    distinguished from slur, x, 29-30
tierce coulée, 89n

time beating: see beating time
time signatures, xiii-xix, 32-47, 100, *114*
    and inequality, 25R, 46
    change of, 46
    chart of, 33, 43n
    definition of, 33
    examples of, 34-5
    inaccurate use of, xiii-xiv, 45
    most commonly used, 39
    relationship to tempo of, xiv-xix, 33, 35-9, 42-5, *114*
    types of, 42-3

    unusual, 42-3R
time words, xvii, 44-5, 93, *111*, *124*
transposition, 67-9, 79-80, 100
tremblements, 75, 76-82, 83, 89, 97, 98, 99, 100-1, 102-5, *112-14*, *116*, *117*, *118-21*
    d'Anglebert's, 81, *117*, *120*
    fingering of, 76-7R, 102-5, *113*
    speed of, 76, 77, 99
    tremblement et pincé, 81-2, *117*, *120*
    with accidentals, x, 78-80, 99

voices (of a composition), 48-50